Match Fishing

MATCH FISHING
The Winner's Peg

PAUL DENNIS

The Crowood Press

First published in 1989 by
The Crowood Press
Ramsbury, Marlborough,
Wiltshire SN8 2HE

British Library Cataloguing in Publication Data
Dennis, Paul
  Match fishing : winners peg.
  1. Coarse fish. Angling. Matches. Manuals
  I. Title
  799.1'1

  ISBN 1–85223–204–8

For Trish and Sammy

Acknowledgements

Photographs by Alan Dawes, Paul Dennis and
Trish Dennis
Line-drawings by Chris Turnbull

Typeset by Footnote Graphics, Warminster, Wilts
Printed in Great Britain by The Bath Press

Contents

Foreword

Having bought this book I would imagine that you want to improve your angling ability. Whether you do improve or not, I am sure that you will find the book full of interesting tips and hints that cannot help but make your fishing much more enjoyable. All of the anglers that contributed their time, knowledge and experience throughout the book are personal friends of mine. They are also proven and consistent winners on the very hard open match circuit of the present day.

Perhaps their exploits, triumphs, and failures, may inspire you to emulate them. I sincerely hope so.

Frank Barlow

Introduction

It is fair to say that the last fifteen years has seen an increase in the average level of angling competence which far outstrips that of any previous era of the sport. In match angling particularly, the level of ability is so great that a very high percentage of the field in any match is possessed of the technical ability to win. That the wins are not evenly spread, and the majority remain, frustratingly, just that good draw away from success, is one of the mysteries of the sport. The law of averages should see all of the anglers winning some of the time; but the fact that some of the anglers win all

A pole winder anchor. Yet another small, but significant, advance in angling bits and pieces. What did we do without them? I can't remember!

of the time has been the same throughout match angling history. There have always been those anglers whose consistency has kept them head and shoulders above the run of the mill. The reasons why some anglers are able to keep ahead may change through the years, however.

Twenty years ago the match angler in the top rank would still make a lot of his own tackle – not the major items, but the small and rather more important ones, such as floats and swingtips – the commercial products in those days being decidedly inferior. Now the general standard of what is available to the match angler across the counter has improved dramatically, as has the choice. Many of the top anglers still make their own floats, but there are plenty more who win, and win well, with shop-bought ones. That is not to suggest that some of the old masters achieved their success simply on the basis of having access to better tackle. The likes of Billy Lane, Jim Sharp, Freddie Foster and Benny Ashurst would have been winners, in any era, on ability alone. Their mastery of the purely mechanical aspects of angling set them apart from the anglers of their day. Their tackle control and technique was such that, for the most part, they were fishing for fish that had never seen an angler's bait before.

Their supremacy can be illustrated by a couple of quick examples. For instance, when the swingtip first came on to the scene it revolutionised ledgering for bream. Very soon most match anglers had a swingtip rod of sorts and, in theory, were in with a chance of winning using this method. Unfortunately they had scant hope of competing with anglers of the calibre of Freddie Foster, because he knew what he was doing with it and they didn't. He had practised long and hard on the method. I started to teach myself the rudiments of swingtipping for bream about fifteen years ago, when the method had been around for a long time. I had plenty of literature and the exploits of Ivan Marks, whose wins and methods were documented down to the last detail, to help me. It still took me two years' hard work, practising five nights a week in the summer, to become proficient in the method.

Similarly, Benny Ashurst was one of the anglers responsible for bringing the caster to match anglers' attention. It took time but eventually they were available to every match angler from local tackle shops. Benny still enjoyed a phenomenal advantage, however, because he understood how the bait behaved in the water and how the fish reacted to it. He realised, almost before anyone else, that it was possible to fish for four hours catching very little, only to destroy the match in the last hour as the fish switched on to the bait. The majority of anglers did not have his patience, and could not understand what was happening. When the caster became a more instant bait he was still ahead of the pack because he had caught fish more often, and for longer, on the bait and knew how to anticipate each change of feeding pattern by recognising familiar signs. He even knew whether to deepen off or shallow up by looking at the position of the hook in the fish's mouth.

Of course these anglers would have found it harder to achieve the same level of consistency today, but the above examples give some clue as to why I believe they would still achieve it. They were leaders of

Even now I still make some of my own floats. These are Lignum-stemmed stick floats. Ideal for fishing at distance, they cast like bullets.

trends, not the followers. They put a great deal of thought, planning, and experimentation into their angling and, by doing so, managed to keep ahead of the crowd.

The four anglers that I have chosen as subjects for this book are all consistent money winners, yet all have very different personalities, outlooks and indeed, angling preferences. I hope that these differences might highlight the common factors which lead to consistency, missing from the majority of anglers on the open match circuit. Without giving too much away, one thing that I did learn was that the 'luck of the draw' had little to do with their winning. They did not draw the out and out fliers and seldom drew where they most fancied but they often seemed able to make things happen. How? Read on.

A genuine Ian Heaps sliding float. Ian gave it to me in return for one of my home-made stick floats. I am still waiting for the slider to turn me into a World Champion!

1 Why?

Angling is a constantly changing sport, with match angling often at the forefront of change. New technology comes along and rods and reels are made ever lighter and more responsive. The pure mechanics of angling are made easier. Finer, more supple lines are developed and these, along with more forgiving rods, smaller but sharper hooks and the enhanced bait presentation that they bring, have witnessed fish being caught in increasing numbers from a variety of venues. Some of these have improved too, with water becoming cleaner and fish stocks flourishing.

In recent years, however, it seems that fish are becoming more difficult to catch on a high proportion of venues, forcing anglers to use ultra-fine line and size 22 and 24 hooks as the norm. Unfortunately this becomes self-defeating, for if the fish cannot trust a bait presented on a size 24 or 26, what can they trust? Anglers have also studied the species balance of venues, and what kind of conditions suit them best. They may work out a particular method or style, sometimes down to aiming it at one particular species, and then try to find a venue that will respond to their favoured tactic. When some anglers discovered that they could draw fish from appreciable distances away by the tactic of loose feeding bronze maggots heavily it revolutionised their fishing. Match angling being what it is, however, it was not too long before this became the main line of attack for all their competitors and, not surprisingly, the method became less effective.

However, the anglers with a bit of imagination about them decided to recreate the environment that first faced them when maggot fishing began to take off. In short, they looked for venues where caster bait was still dominant. By raiding this type of venue, their method still enjoyed much of its initial impact, and once again the minority enjoyed the majority of wins.

More recently there has been the bloodworm revolution of 'balling it in' on canals. This tactic mirrors the heavy continental style and it can have a devastating effect on venues where it has not become the norm and there are plenty of fish. Again, the anglers that feel most confident on this method are constantly searching for venues that have not seen the approach and where the majority of anglers will not tend to use it.

Sometimes anglers become associated with one particular method or technique, and once its effectiveness wears off, as it is certain to do in time, they fade from the scene. However, there are some anglers who will rise to prominence at such times, and remain there because of their adaptability to change and these are always the anglers who are hardest to beat. As stated earlier, the average standard of match angling ability is probably the highest that it has ever been and I would estimate that on any given match, 90 per cent of the field could win given a decent draw. In spite of this there are anglers who are consistent winners and those who are not. I would class myself in the latter category.

That notwithstanding, I am obviously fascinated by what makes the consistent anglers so successful. When they do have a run of good pegs it often seems to go on forever and they are among the big money winners the season through. In between times they are usually also still picking up here and there, ticking over very nicely. At one time, a few years ago now, I felt that I was flirting with the big league. I went out on the open circuit and began the long and tortuous route to the match angling summit.

In those naive days (a good fifteen years ago now), I firmly believed that I would one day be good enough to fish for England at World Championship level. I was hungry for success. I believed that every time I failed to win anything I had made a mistake and that the peg must have been worth a lot more. I certainly did not fall into the trap of blaming the draw bag for every set back and I worked long and hard to perfect what techniques were available then.

I was encouraged by anglers like Tony Scott, then an England International and a local lad made good. In terms of technical ability, I could hold my own with most in my neighbourhood, although I won with less regularity than some of them. I discovered later that some were just natural anglers, almost impossible to beat when they landed on a few fish. Their instincts did most of the hard work for them. However, there were also the Tony Scotts of this world, by no means natural anglers but, so technically precise and analytical that they were able to bridge that gap with ease. If I couldn't be a natural, at least I could become a technician.

I travelled the country fishing a wide variety of venues and won a fair amount of respect, most of it, it must be said, on venues distant from my home. I remembered the old saying about 'A prophet in his own land'. I was not afraid to experiment.

Thirteen years ago I came fourth in a rain-affected Long Higgin Open by fishing with a roach pole. I practised any method that I thought might give me an edge. The same year, I won a club match on the River Trent by switching to a size 22 hook to 0.22kg nylon, picking up a few extra dace.

One season, about eleven years ago, my wanderings took me south and I met a couple of anglers who presented me with a golden opportunity to achieve my aims. Through Mark Downes and Pete Hobson I joined the Starlets, then beginning to flex their muscles in well-publicised winter league campaigns against Colton Hackett. I was accepted into the squad as an equal. I had talents which they felt were needed, also a different viewpoint on some things. Eventually I made by debut in a winter league match and won my section. I felt that I was on my way, but still I was not reaping the rewards I felt I should in open matches.

Most of the other squad members had open results far better than mine, yet it was accepted that my turn would come. They were less impatient than I was. However, I felt it difficult to justify my place in such company if I could not come up with results. I kept on practising, especially on the River Trent around Nottingham. At one stage I experimented with groundbait and squatts in an attempt to fish the waggler further out than catapulted loose feed would reach. One notable match it worked. I drew in the dead man's bay area and won the section comfortably. Having under-estimated the size of my catch quite outrageously, I was told by the scalesman that I was as bad as Frank Barlow. I took that as a compliment.

The same year, I used the squatt and groundbait method to take fourth place in a 300-peg CEGB match on the Trent at Shelford. I drew opposite the road stretch and had a catch which included just about

Tony Scott in action on the Trent and Mersey Canal, very close to a peg where I had an open match win. In fact, the angler closer to the road bridge is on the very spot.

everything – bream, carp, chub, roach, gudgeon, bleak, perch, even a rudd and a couple of dace. However, the big win on the method never came. I used to go and practise on the river in that area even though the fishing was better and easier in my own neck of the woods. I reasoned that if I could catch fish there, I could catch them anywhere.

One glorious day I caught over thirteen kilos of roach on the waggler from the pegs in the reeds opposite the Stoke Ferry Inn. I managed to draw there once when there was about an extra half metre of water on and a facing gale. Again, I had that tantalising glimpse of future glory when I won a

Trentman Badge. I was second in A zone, Shelford. The Starlets team that I was in came sixth – a good performance.

Occasionally, it would look as if I was about to embark upon a winning run. I won a canal open at Stretton from a peg that is seldom put in these days right on the concrete on the Hillfield side of the road bridge. I alternated between casters fished on rod and line for roach, and a four-metre pole and bloodworm for gudgeon. I weighed in a kilo and had plenty to spare over the runner-up. A few days later, I drew a fairly nondescript peg on the River Trent at Bladon. I had a method worked out for those pegs and started on it. It

Left to Right: Nigel Bull, Tony Scott, Paul Dennis, Robin Banton. Tony decided on the team name 'The Four Just Men'. We won the BJAC summer league three times in the first four years that it was fished. The year that we didn't win it, we came second.

involved fishing a seven-metre pole to hand with caster on the hook over a bed of a couple of litres of hemp. In practice it had worked like a dream. In the match I caught one tiny roach in fifteen minutes hard work. I switched to the conventional stick float rig and had a really lucky break as I hooked and landed a barbel of a kilo and a half. Once I had removed that from the swim I went on to take a nice net of roach,

eventually weighing in five kilos to take second place. There was a terrible downstream wind that day and it was one of my best ever performances on the stick float. That run lasted for two matches.

A local summer league was formed to work out the potential of the rapidly improving Trent in the Burton town area. I was invited to join a team which included Tony Scott, Nigel Bull and Robin Banton.

We won the league three times out of the first four it was fished and a couple of times subsequently, although the personnel had changed a little by then. One year I had an unbelievable run, taking first, second, third and fifth in the forty peg sections, to add the individual points title to our team success. But it seemed as though these were the only matches that I was doing well in at that juncture.

As a squad of what were, basically, river anglers we also had a go at the canal winter league that was set up around that time, achieving a notable double of summer and winter league titles in the same year. I began to suspect that team fishing was really my strong point. Myself, Derek Jackson, Dave Bird and Pete Hobson put a team in to the Rye Super four-team match one year. We didn't just win it, we destroyed a good-class field, pulling 190 points out of a possible 200. We had ABC and Dorking trailing in our wake.

From time to time, I would beat not just good but great anglers off the next peg, but never when there was any chance of winning anything. Perhaps they were just going through the motions. I remember narrowly beating Dennis White on the Wharfe at Tadcaster, only for him to massacre me on the Trent at Burton Joyce a couple of years later. I got the better of Dickie Carr on the Rother in Kent on one notable match, but we were in a difficult area. On fish, it might have been different. I have even been drawn next to Johnny Moult on four occasions and we are even at two all. However, when he has beaten me, he has finished in the frame; when I have beaten him, it hasn't really mattered.

I should have won some matches that I only did well in. One which still haunts me was an open match on my local stretch of the River Trent. It had attracted a brilliant field of anglers – Clive Smith, Ken Giles, Frank Barlow, Wayne Swinscoe, John Allerton. It was a real who's who of match angling.

I drew a breamy area that hadn't shown too much recent form. In fact the week previously, 280 grams had come off it. I decided to fish for bream though and fed it with groundbait. To cut a long story short, I began to catch well during the middle of the match, but had gone so long waiting for bites that I decided to stay on a size 20 hook. In the fair current of the upper Trent I lost nearly as many as I landed but didn't even consider switching up a size or two. I am sure the fish wouldn't have minded. I finished second to Roy Duckett. I should have won that match by a street. I will never have a better opportunity to beat a field of that class of angler.

The nearest that I have come to that kind of performance since, was in one of the Wednesday Opens on the river at Burton. I won a section that contained Clive Smith, Tony Scott and Kevin Ashurst among others. It didn't escape my notice that I tended to do better in these mid-week matches, against high class fields, than I was doing at the weekends, against lesser ones. Obviously, mid-week fishing on the Trent is far easier than weekend fishing. It is the same for everyone. What tends to happen is that there are a few fish to be caught from everywhere mid-week, and this is not the case at the weekend.

Another of my better performances was in a two-day festival match on the Newbridge to Iden length of the River Rother. Graciously put up by Dave Bird, I was in an ideal frame of mind for these matches and, as the two dates coincided with the first two days of the season, I was in with just as much chance as anyone else.

The first day I drew second peg away from the Iden end of the match length – supposedly a good area, but one which I had not fished before. I picked up a couple of small fish on the waggler in the first half

I landed this fish safely enough, but lost too many others and could only come second to Goole's Roy Duckett. If I had won this match, my match angling career might have been very different.

A couple of insert wagglers of the type that I used on the first day of the Rye Super 2. Although they tend to take less shot than a bodied waggler, they also offer less resistance to the current and can therefore be controlled more easily. On a relatively narrow venue such as the Rother, they allowed me to reach the required distance with ease.

hour when the sluices were opened and the river began to run off. Although it seemed to be going through at a fair lick, it was actually quite steady compared to venues like the Trent so I was well equipped to cope. On went a heavier waggler which, well undershotted, I was able to ease through the swim quite nicely.

The only drawback was that my loose feed was obviously going to struggle to hit bottom within the confines of my swim, but I plugged away and picked up a couple of nice roach, one nudging the half-kilo mark. To rest the swim I switched to a straight ledger, and again was lucky. A small carp and a reasonable eel came to this rig and, with the addition of another few

waggler-caught fish, I came fourth on day one with a catch just short of two and a half kilos. I was about half a kilo adrift of the leading angler.

Day two saw me draw an area not renowned for decent catches and the only advice given to me was to fish for bleak. Nevertheless, I still had the previous day's match in my system and believed that I could pick up bonus fish from anywhere. This proved not to be the case and I wasted time fishing for non-existent fish. However, I had set a pole rig up for the bleak which, by today's standards, will probably seem a little crude. One concession to finesse was a size 22 hook and 0.23kg hooklink. I set the float to fish at one metre. No fish were topping so there seemed little point in fishing greased-line tactics. A couple of micros down the line to help the bait sink were the only additions to this rig.

I found that I could pick up bleak fairly steadily by dotting around the swim, picking up a few here and there rather than concentrating on one spot. However, I could not believe that I would do any good by sticking to this so it was a case of back to the waggler for another fishless period. This time I put the rod right up the bank out of reach, in order that I wouldn't be tempted to waste more time on the method. I decided to see the match out on the pole.

The bait that I was using was a single squatt. In practice in previous seasons I had found that I could get bites on squatts a lot more quickly than when I fished with a pinkie on the hook. Bleak continued to come steadily and I had to make the minimum of depth changes to search them out. The five-metre pole that I was using gave me enough reach. In the latter stages I began to pick up a few tiny roach and skimmer bream in with the bleak, the constant activity of the bleak probably

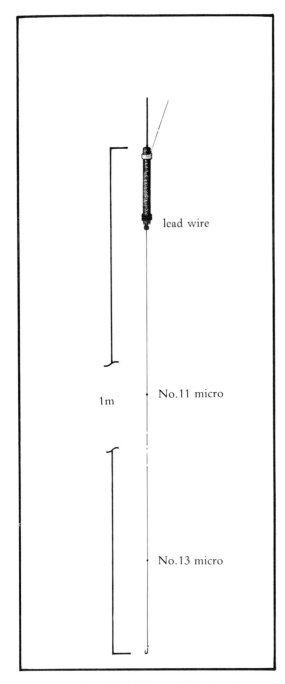

lead wire

1m

No.11 micro

No.13 micro

Fine Sarkandas reed pole float used for sub-surface bleak fishing on the River Rother.

spurring them into feeding. I began to wish that I had fished for bleak from start to finish. The bites were coming just as well at the end as at the start.

I had been told prior to the start that a kilo of bleak would be the absolute maximum that I could expect. I weighed in a kilo and a half having wasted a lot of time not fishing for them. However, the catch gave me third on the day and second place overall behind bleak ace Ray Mumford who had just under a kilo advantage. This was obviously another match that had got away from me but, looking at some of the anglers whom I did beat, I didn't do too badly. I beat Stan Piecha for the section on day two and had Steve Gardener behind me in the overall list on that day as well. Just look how they have prospered. In the same match a year later I managed to pinch the section from Dickie Carr who was drawn on the next peg. Two pegs away from him was John McCarthy. I was starting to move in quite exclusive circles.

I was travelling around the country quite a bit at this stage and thought nothing of making the six-hour trek down to Kent for a weekend's fishing. My angling was improving because of it. One strange factor that I did notice was that the techniques that I had worked so slavishly to perfect on my home venues, which were bringing me scant reward there, seemed to work a treat in foreign parts. I was very resistant to the local methods and tried to do my own thing wherever possible – something that I still favour. The shock of the new can sometimes bring brilliant results.

No matter how well I did, though, it never seemed to be enough. I was very self critical, possibly a little too critical. Around that time it was fashionable for some of the top anglers to say that they didn't mind being beaten off the next peg so long as it was on a day when they were in with no chance of winning the match.

Second in the Rye Super 2 event on the River Rother at Iden Lock. Ray Mumford bleaked his way to victory.

Obviously, this was intended to diminish the achievements of lesser mortals who had the temerity to take them on. Some of them made it sound as if they could *never* be beaten if they pulled all the stops out. I certainly didn't subscribe to this theory and used to take it as an insult if I was beaten by an adjacent angler. Getting beaten on both sides had me reaching for the razor blades. I was inconsolable.

So, I was enjoying a few minor successes here and there, I had gained the respect of my fellow anglers and there was every

chance that I might make it to the top. So what went wrong? That isn't as facetious a question as it might seem. It is as important to find out what the top anglers don't do as it is to find out what they do do.

I think that I made a few elementary mistakes along the way which set me off on the wrong road. One of these was being seduced into fishing venues that did not suit me. Some of them were very, very peggy and this was the last thing that I needed. What little talent I did have was given no chance to blossom under those

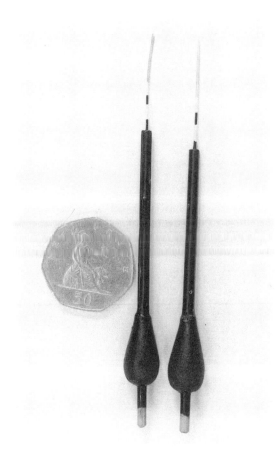

Running line bleak floats. I made these up for the River Rother after I came second in the Rye Super 2. Another case of closing the stable door after the horse had bolted.

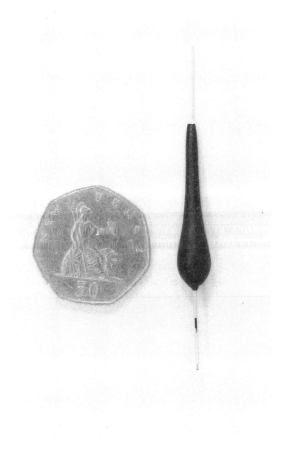

This was another attempt at a sub-surface bleak float for the Rother. More sophisticated than the sarkandas reed job, and, dare I say it, ahead of its time shape-wise.

conditions and, more importantly, I had no real bench mark, under those conditions, to measure my progress against. I don't know why, but I let myself be talked into fishing venues like the middle Ouse and the upper Thames – not really venues which would improve my prospects. Also, if I had done well there, who would have known?

Another fault, perhaps, was that I fished too many matches, not allowing myself enough time to practise, with the result that I lacked the confidence to catch a big net of fish when the opportunity presented itself. I was also constantly facing situations in matches which had never occurred in what practice I had done. Open matches are an expensive learning ground.

However, this was not always the case. There was a time, early on, when I did put in a lot of practice. I remember drawing a very difficult peg at Clifton Grove on one match and taking three hours to sort it out. I tried a short pole for gudgeon – catch rate: twelve a minute, six a minute, four a minute, nil a minute, snag. A heavy balsa, the peg was very deep, fast and boily under my own bank – catch: a few roach, a couple of tiny chub and one or two bleak. Eventually I tried the waggler.

About four rod lengths out, the river shallowed and slowed. I decided to try this area. A couple of decent chub came to me straight away and then nothing. I finished up fishing three metres deep in one metre of water, holding the rod high to keep the line out of the fast water as much as I could, but still having to pay off line like crazy to stop the float from dragging out of the catching area too quickly. I weighed in seven kilos and got into the frame. A few days later I drove the forty miles over to that venue after work. Fishing it properly I caught fifteen kilos in a couple of hours. I suppose that I began to think that I knew it all then and stopped going to practise.

Another factor that stopped me going was my very lack of success. I knew that I was drawing badly on a lot of the matches that I was fishing, and it came to the point where I thought that practice was useless – I was never going to get the opportunity to display my talents. Successful travelling companions made things even worse. Not just once, but several times, I have returned from venues biteless and broke with companions who had been beaten on one or even two sides and still won their sections. I always seemed to be in the section with a couple of anglers too many or the one with the bonus chub. (I never caught it.) Whenever I got beaten at the next peg the anglers didn't make the frame.

Drawing badly did give me plenty of opportunity to walk the banks and see the real stars in action and, as I was fishing a lot of matches at Burton Joyce in those days, there was no shortage of them. I tried hard to see what they did, and picked up some useful pointers but the things that they were doing didn't seem to work on some of the pegs that I was drawing. Maybe I

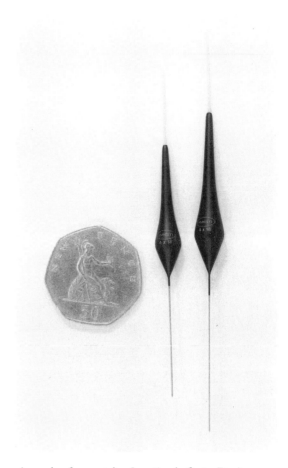

A couple of present-day Ignesti pole floats. Don't they look a bit familiar?

wasn't doing them in the right way. In retrospect, I should have tried what I saw on pegs where it would have worked.

My angling progress had come to a halt. Anglers who I was once on a par with were now far ahead of me. I had not been able to stand the pace. I realised that the big break never comes for some anglers and resigned myself to being one of them. Progression is everything in angling. Methods change very quickly and to stay at the top, an angler has to almost anticipate those changes. This can only be done through practice. However, as I found out, unless

Tackling up for the Division One National on the upper Trent. I drew a piece of water that I know quite well, and was told that I was on a flier. I wasn't, I was about thirty metres downstream of it and on a rather poor area. I couldn't think of anything to smile about.

the end result is positive in terms of match results, how is the angler to know that the practice is doing him any good?

Eventually, I decided to please myself and I like to think that I was in good company in this respect because John Dean came to the same conclusion. I decided to fish where and when I wanted to and tried to pick venues that interested me. I was still hungry for success but I was a little less frantic about it.

The first season that I decided to turn over a new leaf I won my first match of the season with twenty kilos of chub. Unfortunately, by the end of the season I was back on the treadmill again, but this time I realised the futility of trying to make something happen by sheer persistence of attendance. After all, I already knew that it was possible to fish a twenty odd series of matches without so much as a section pick-up from the first time around, so why should I have expected anything different the second time? My next 'dropping out' was much more successful.

So, what has my history of failure got to do with open match success? How not to do it? Dead right! As I said earlier, I had the opportunity to watch some brilliant anglers in action, and I did watch them, but I wasn't *seeing* anything. To me, they looked the same as I did, but they were on better pegs catching lots of fish. This was totally wrong.

Most of the top men have spent long hours watching other anglers in action absorbing, like a sponge, the good and bad points of their styles. Some spend years doing this before venturing out on to the open circuit themselves. This book gave me another crack at the whip, and also a chance to impart the knowledge of what to look for. I feel sure that there are plenty of anglers in the same position as I was in – looking but not seeing.

My trek got me out on the open circuit again, rubbing shoulders with top anglers. Although it had been years since I had met some of them, they seemed genuinely glad to see me. I hope that it was not just because I represented easy pools fodder! I visited a variety of venues, some of which posed problems that I hadn't planned for. In that respect, I was back to square one. I had intended to practise with the anglers concerned in an attempt to iron out some of the more serious faults. Unfortunately, this was not possible in most cases. These anglers' schedules were already busy enough. That they did manage to help me at all speaks volumes for them and their desire to put something back into the sport, potentially at the expense of some of their match winnings.

Who knows, it may be that I will stumble across something which may fit all the pieces of the puzzle together for some angler, who may then beat them at their own game. One thing I can tell you now, without spoiling what is to come, is that if that angler is you, and you do beat them at their own game, don't expect to be able to rest on your laurels. Even as you do they will have taken that one pace ahead again!

2 Nigel Bull

Nigel is probably the least nationally known angler in this book, even though he has a fine reputation on a wide variety of venues. His list of placings encompasses venues as varied and distant as the River Welland, where he had a third placing in the National Championship, and the swifter flowing River Trent, where he has enjoyed great success. The River Thames is a venue which holds no terrors for him, as is the Warwickshire Avon.

Probably the greatest contrast in styles is illustrated by his love for the big-weight matches in Ireland, where he has won the prestigious Sealink Classic (one of the richest events in the calendar), and his keenness to fish canals. Obviously, more modest winning weights are expected of the latter, but perhaps they are closer to the top-class Irish venues than might be expected. On either venue, an angler catching steadily might expect at least 300 fish in a five-hour match, which is not particularly fast, in match fishing terms. However, at the end of the day, the angler in Ireland would possibly be looking for forty kilos while the canal angler would be happy with a mere four kilos (although that would be an exceptional weight on the majority of canals!).

At 36 years of age, Nigel is the youngest angler covered here. However, he has worked his way into a job which gives him plenty of opportunity to go fishing and he seems to have been around the match circuit for ever. Because of this he has picked up a wealth of experience beyond his years.

In common with a good many match anglers, his first involvement with competitive angling came in the form of club matches – especially the away matches where he enjoyed the opportunity to try different techniques.

This level of competition led to higher things and happily, this coincided with the recovery of his local River Trent. Once heavily polluted, it was becoming clean again by the early 1970s. Living in Willington, Nigel was able to take advantage of that section's return to form, which rather preceded the rest of the river thanks to the well-oxygenated waters of the River Dove which join the River Trent at Newton Solney, a few miles upstream of Willington.

Derby Angling Association owns the fishing rights to the vast majority of the waters on the Trent around Willington, and it was not long before Nigel became involved with their National Championship teams – the start of his interest in team fishing. However, Nigel's real rise began when the River Trent began to clean up above the influence of the River Dove. For a few years there existed that tenuous balance between pollution and cleanliness which seems to attract fish (particularly roach), like a magnet. It seemed as if almost every fish in the river was determined to reach the very edge of the clean water and, not surprisingly, the Swadlincote waters on the River Trent at Bladon became an angling Mecca.

Top anglers from all over the Midlands were eager to fish the venue, and every

England International, Tony Scott, was a source of inspiration to Nigel Bull, especially in matches on the River Trent. Here, Tony displays a net of fish from the embankment at Nottingham.

Former Coventry captain, Bob Eaton, with another match winning catch. This time, dace from the River Dove. He also made a prize catch by signing Nigel Bull up for National Championship duty.

match was sure to be a sell out. One of the most consistent anglers on the venue at that time was England International, Tony Scott, acknowledged as one of the most technically correct anglers in the country. Tony's drive for perfection had a profound influence on Nigel, as did his keen analysis of fishes' feeding patterns.

Nigel's deceptively casual nature often belies his drive for success – something that has made him into one of the hardest working anglers on the open circuit. The upper Trent is a venue of fickle moods, and a wide variety of swims, all of which can require specialised knowledge to tackle – a surprisingly good training ground for the apparently more simple techniques of canal fishing.

This Trent training also gave Nigel the confidence to spread his wings on the open match circuit and visit ever more distant venues. Obviously not all of them responded to the methods in which he was well schooled, but this only made him more determined to succeed.

Eventually the wins started to come, and naturally his versatility meant that he was in demand as a team angler. The quest for anglers with fresh ideas saw him joining Coventry for a few seasons, and it is from here that his canal interest stems. However, he was soon picked up by Coleshill in their attempt on the Division One National on the upper Trent. Nigel linked up with Tony Scott again.

Most recently, Nigel has been associated with the DAM Starlets team, a decision that he has never regretted. Here it was not just his angling ability that attracted attention, but also his ability to read a venue. Starlets brought him in as expert adviser for a crucial match on the upper Trent, and his in-depth knowledge of the venue helped them to a crushing victory. This, coupled with a timely win in the Sealink made Starlets' skipper, Mark Downes'

mind up, and Nigel was invited to join an already strong squad.

The brisk interchange of ideas that flows through such a talented collection of anglers was immediately attractive to Nigel, as was the opportunity to try to force his way into their team. Undoubtedly, this association with one of the country's top teams has further enhanced Nigel's reputation but he maintains his place in the squad on merit and is rated as one of their top all-round anglers.

Although canal fishing is a specialised art, it is increasing in popularity, and canals that at one time never saw an angler from one year to the next are now the venues for sell-out open matches. One of the reasons for this is that canals are apparently fair venues, especially in the eyes of the anglers who are most successful on them! I cannot entirely share this view, especially as those same anglers are still keen to get what they feel is a good draw and bemoan their fate if they are unlucky enough to pick a bad one. However, I can see their point that the usually more modest weights required to win canal matches mean that the chasing pack are rarely too far adrift of the winners. Also, unlike most river venues, one big bonus fish, which could turn up from even the most unfancied peg, can put the angler in with a winning chance.

Perhaps my view that canals are not really fair venues is coloured by the fact that canals are traditionally thought of as places for anglers to go in the winter. This is possibly the worst time to visit them. At that time of year canals can become very patchy, with high concentrations of fish in one area and virtually none in others. Summer too, brings problems in the shape of boats and there are few canals which do not suffer to a degree from heavy traffic of this nature. The perfect compromise is, naturally enough, autumn, but even then falling leaves can be a problem!

By now I have probably succeeded in convincing you that I hate canals. This is not true; I enjoy canal fishing. What I cannot accept is that they are the wonderfully fair venues that some anglers would have you believe. There will always be some swims that hold more fish than others, just as there will always be some anglers more capable of taking their opportunities than others.

Nigel's chosen venue was the Trent and Mersey Canal – quite a picturesque venue as canals go, and as local to me as it is to him. Although I have had nowhere near the success on the venue that Nigel has enjoyed, I have managed to win the odd match here and there, especially when being fortunate enough to draw one of the supposedly non-existent fliers!

Nigel's consistency hinted at rather more than mere good fortune at the draw bag, however, and I was keen to see, at first hand, those attributes that made him so effective. August Bank Holiday weekend was the chosen time for our canal fishing sessions, with a couple of open matches, organised by the Burton Mutual AA being taken in. The first match was pegged on the Stretton length, the scene of my first ever match win. In those unsophisticated times I only needed a quartet of roach for a few grams. Rather more would be needed this time.

Stretton is a split section either side of a road bridge and strangely, on such an impartial venue, most of the anglers wanted to be drawn below the bridge towards the Clay Mills end. Unfortunately, Nigel didn't manage to drop on the area that he most fancied, and had to settle for peg 25, two above the bridge – a far from noted area. Far bank cover was non-existent which was particularly bad news. The reason for this is that such pegs are more subject to the disturbing influences of the myriad boats that ply the canal. A decent protruding bit of far bank cover gives the fish somewhere to hide, and encourages the boats to keep to the very centre of the canal. It can sometimes (though rarely), encourage them to slow down a little too.

The fish that Nigel hoped to base the bulk of his catch around were roach – small fish in the thirty to fifty gram range, with an odd one or two around the hundred gram mark. His main bait was to be bloodworm used with bloodworm and joker feed, although he also had a back up that had potential to turn his peg into a match winner. The ace in the hole was hemp seed – a bait which can, on its day, drive roach into near frenzy. It also tends to attract a far

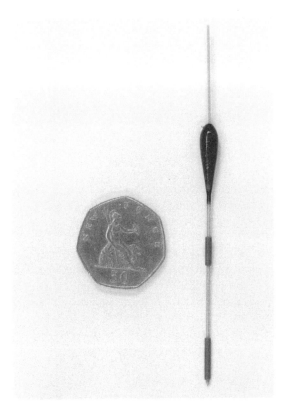

One of the range of Dick Clegg pole floats. This size and shape is a particular favourite of Nigel Bull's for far-bank fishing.

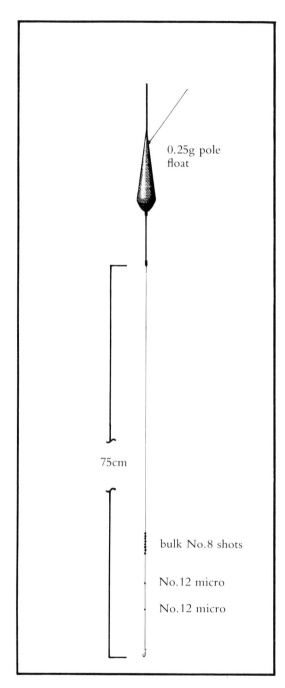

0.25g pole
float

75cm

bulk No.8 shots

No.12 micro

No.12 micro

Nigel Bull's 'standard' short pole rig.

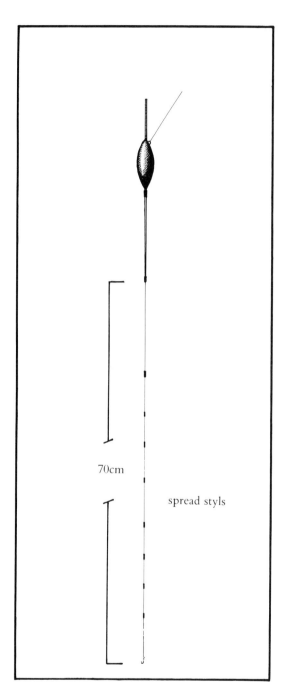

70cm

spread styls

*Barbetta fly float rig used by Nigel Bull on the
Trent and Mersey Canal.*

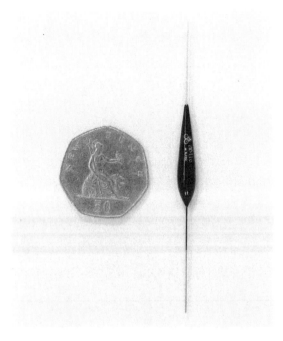

This is the type of float that Nigel Bull favours for most of his close-in work on the Trent and Mersey Canal. A 0.25g Milo Eris.

larger stamp of fish than more normal canal baits.

Nigel tackled up two rigs for the match – one a one-and-a-half metre pole for near side work, the other a long pole for the far shelf of the canal. A 0.25g float shaped like an inverted pear drop was set up on the short pole. The terminal tackle was set up with conventional split shot bunched a few centimetres away from the hook with a couple of micro shot as droppers below this. The shots gave more versatility than the normal choice of an olivette lead, obviously more adjustable to the whims of the fish. Gudgeon were the main quarry for this rig, although it was unlikely that they would provide enough weight to win the match in their own right. However, the half kilo or so of weight that they might add to the final total would increase Nigel's chances of winning.

A near side swim also allowed Nigel the opportunity to rest his far bank swim whilst still keeping a catch rate of sorts going. The short line would be the first to be fished as results would be fairly instant and Nigel would rapidly be able to assess the worth of staying with that line or switching to his main line of attack, the far bank. The tackle set up for the far bank was very different to that for the near side. A very much lighter 0.15g Barbetta Fly float was used on this rig. Again this was a balsa on wire float but of a different shape, being similar to a conventional Avon float. Knowing of Nigel's normal preference for even lighter balsa on cane floats, I asked why he had chosen this pattern. His initial reply was that he just liked the look of the float, and the wire stem might add a touch of stability on what was developing into a very windy day.

Both pole rigs were completed by size 24 hooks to 0.34kg nylon, although the shotting on the far bank rig was very different. A string of tiny Styl leads allowed a slow dropping bait presentation, with only the fine bristle showing when the leads had settled completely. Having the tackles ready assembled on winders allowed Nigel the luxury of several minutes plumbing the depth of his swim in order to familiarise himself with the contours of the canal bed. The classic cross-section of a canal as depicted in most writings can be very misleading. Not all canals are the same and there can be a huge variation in the underwater features of adjacent swims. This could be a reason why fish will sometimes tend to favour certain areas even though the bankside features seem to be similar.

Nigel's peg had the textbook canal cross-section – a far bank and near bank shelf around a metre and a half wide with about three-quarters of a metre's depth. The centre channel was not plumbed as, with the level of boat traffic expected, it was

Gudgeon can be vital make-weights on the canal, and even match winners in their own right. Paul Crouch lands a gudgeon taken at three metres on the Trent and Mersey Canal.

unlikely that many fish would be taking up residence in that part of the swim. However, the drop-off point of the far shelf was mentally marked as this would be likely to provide most of the fish to fall to the bloodworm hookbait.

I was very interested in Nigel's groundbait mix, as I had heard quite a few rumours as to its heavy nature. His basic mix was very simple and similar to that which I had been using the previous season. An equal 45 per cent mixture of Van Den Eynde Beet and Super Cup groundbaits plus 10 per cent damp leam carried the bloodworm and joker. Three tennis-ball-sized helpings of feed, squeezed very tightly,

were introduced across on to the far shelf at the start of the match.

The near side swim was treated to two balls about the size of a hen's egg, put in less than a metre away from the bank. Nigel's first put in on this line resulted in a bristling perch of a couple of hundred grams or so – a nice way to start the match – and a couple of gudgeon soon joined it in the keepnet. However, the bites soon ceased, and with less than half a dozen fish to show for twenty minute's effort, prospects did not look good for the near side.

A switch to the far bank swim at eleven metres brought an upturn in sport as small roach showed a liking for the delicately

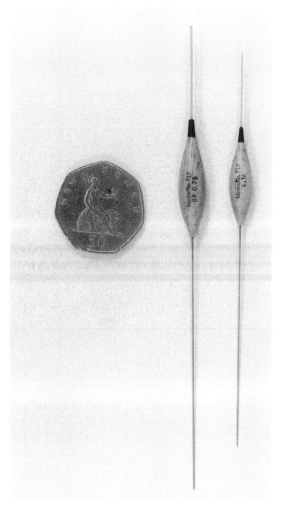

Barbetta fly pole floats. The long wire stem allowed Nigel Bull to present his bait correctly in the very windy conditions. The streamlined body meant that there was less resistance when lifting into a fish.

presented bloodworm. In between un-hooking fish and rebaiting his hook Nigel catapulted hemp seed into his swim. This was introduced slightly downstream of the groundbaited area in order to keep the two swims separate. Although only a couple of metres apart, Nigel pointed out that the two swims were very different – a concept which I found difficult to grasp. He added that introducing the balls of feed slightly

upstream of his angling position, rather than directly in front, did help. I had missed the fact that this was where he had introduced the heavy feed in spite of watching him quite closely.

The amount of hemp that Nigel was introducing was quite an eye-opener. As someone used to feeding less than a quarter of a litre of hemp during a four-hour match I was shocked to see him well on the way to introducing a litre or more in similar time. Nigel has won plenty of canal matches thanks to hemp seed, however, whilst my success on the bait has been limited to practice sessions alone, and then the small amounts that I introduced meant that I had to wait for a long time before the fish accepted the bait. Nigel's feeding technique made more instant results more likely.

Even at this early stage of the match, it was clear that the increasingly strong wind was going to make life very difficult. The more sheltered swims around the garage area would certainly be worth a few extra fish on such a day. Nigel was catching fish in a steady rather than spectacular manner, although they were a smaller stamp than he would have liked. Occasionally, a fish of 150 grams or so was brought to hand, with the remark that this was the correct size to be catching.

To try to increase the size of the fish that he was catching, Nigel switched to a grain of hemp on his size 24 hook. Just over an hour had passed and Nigel was confident that he would attract bites on hemp. He explained that the hemp seed had to be presented much closer to the far bank, right in amongst the grass and weeds. As he predicted, bites came straight away but, perhaps because the strong wind hampered his presentation, the bites were very tenta-tive. The small hook meant that Nigel was struggling to hit the bites, although a change to a larger size could have meant no bites at all, and lessened the effectiveness of

Nigel Bull tackling up for a match on the Trent and Mersey Canal at Stretton.

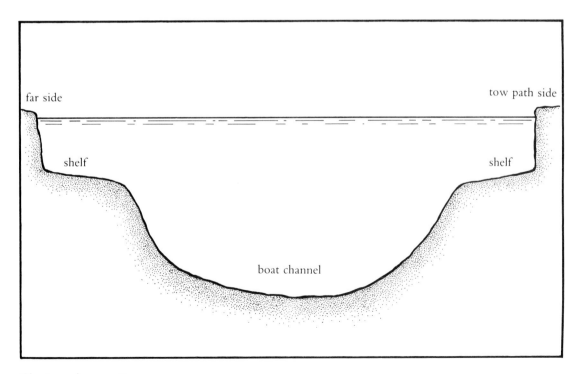

Classic canal cross-section.

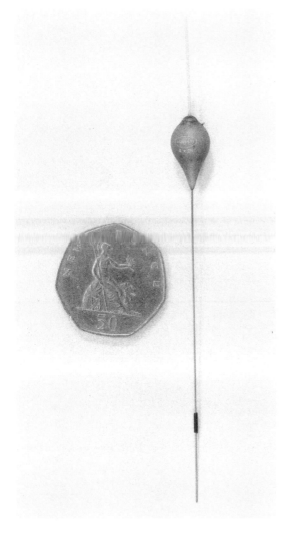

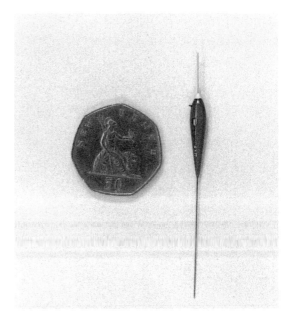

This pattern of float offers a compromise between the Barbetta Fly and the Ignesti floats shown on the preceding pages. However, the bristle is too small and would render the float virtually invisible at eleven or twelve metres.

This Ignesti float also boasts a long wire stem for stability, but the shape of the body is, perhaps, too rounded for canal fishing.

bloodworm on the hook. A spare tip section ready set up with identical tackle save for a larger hook would have been ideal.

It soon became clear that unless the wind lessened in strength Nigel was going to struggle to win the match with hemp seed on the hook, in spite of it bringing him an odd better fish. A slowing down of all bites on the far side prompted Nigel to try the inside swim again. Unfortunately he was unable to attract so much as a bite. At the next peg upstream, Dave Jackson was catching a few fish on his close-in method, although he was fishing about a couple of metres further out than Nigel. His catching rate was slower than Nigel's when fishing the far bank, however, so prospecting for bites on the short pole did not seem to be a winning method either.

Realising that Nigel was going through a slow spell, I decided to take a walk up to the Stretton end of the length to see how the other anglers were faring. Nigel had told me that Tony Scott had drawn on a good area and he would almost certainly be amongst some fish. It seemed that most of the anglers along the tow-path were interested to hear how Nigel was doing, however. Obviously, he was the man to beat in their eyes. Nigel's Starlets team mate, Eddie Coales, was as keen for information as anyone, especially as his own peg was showing signs of deteriorating.

Eddie was set back in a near side bay, which made his swim a good three metres wider than his fourteen-metre pole could reach. This put him at a great disadvantage as the fish could easily drift out of reach into the far bank cover, and be frequently dispersed by the regular boat traffic. Perhaps it is swims like this which give the lie to canals being fair venues.

Only about forty metres away, and with a vacant peg in between, Tony Scott was situated in a very different kind of swim. Two protruding far bank bushes gave the swim plenty of character whilst keeping the boats at bay and a good sized gap in between allowed Tony to fish the pole with ease. The canal also narrowed in this area, with ten metres being more than adequate to reach the far bank.

As Nigel had predicted, Tony was catching well. He had fed his swim very heavily at the outset and was now reaping the rewards. The increases in the rate of flow caused by the opening of the lock gates seemed to encourage a better stamp of roach into feeding, fish of around three hundred grams being common. Picking these up with encouraging regularity, Tony looked a likely winner. Returning to Nigel, I found that he too had picked up a few better fish by persevering with the hemp seed. However, he still had to switch back to bloodworm on the hook to maintain his catching pattern. It was noticeable that while Nigel continued to catch, the anglers around him were struggling for bites.

To my eyes, the difference seemed to be in Nigel's work rate. Rarely was the bait still for long when bloodworm was on the hook. The float was constantly twitched and retrieved slightly, allowing the bait to drift over the edge of the shelf in a

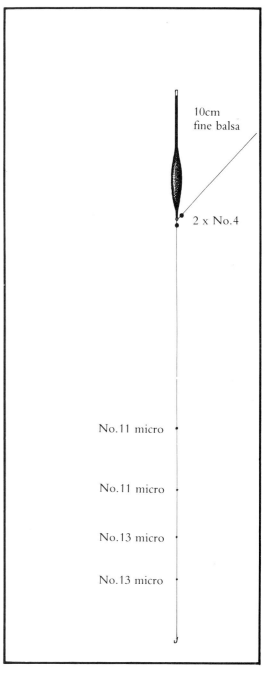

One of Tony Scott's far bank pole rigs. Tony is one of the few anglers to fish the loose float method in conjunction with the long pole. However, he uses it to devastating effect.

Back to his roots and still difficult to beat. Tony Scott on the Trent and Mersey Canal at Stretton.

DAM Starlets' Nigel Bull brings a fish to the net, taken on hemp seed. It was, as he expected, appreciably larger than the bloodworm-caught fish.

natural manner. This constant movement appeared to be the key to success with the bloodworm. Also, Nigel was constantly adjusting the depth at which he was fishing. A centimetre here or there seemed to make all the difference in keeping the fish interested.

The hemp seed was treated rather differently in that it was laid on slightly over-depth in an attempt to attract a slower bite, although Nigel did seem to expect bites on the drop with the hemp if the fish really got going on it. With all of the constant adjustments requiring regular unshipping of the pole it seemed to me that five hours on a canal was even harder work than five hours on a swiftly flowing river.

With just over an hour remaining, I was sent off on another scouting expedition. Tony Scott was catching at a faster rate than previously and looked to have the match sewn up. Eddie Coales' swim had died completely and, to add to his misery, the angler on the other side of him, also on a narrower peg, was catching at a steady rate. However, the majority of the anglers, even in this area, seemed to be struggling. Mostly fishing at four or five metres they did not look to be in with much of a chance of winning.

Continuing his swapping and changing, Nigel managed to keep catching right up to the whistle, although his fish were of a much smaller average size than Tony Scott's, and it didn't look as though he had caught enough of them. However, when the scales arrived there was a major shock in store. One of the anglers apparently catching very little, to the left of Tony Scott, was in fact quietly and efficiently winkling out a very nice net of roach caught at just four metres. Burton's Pete Wagstaffe literally stole the match with 3kg 113g, while Tony Scott had to settle for second with 2kg 886g. Another reasonable roach would have won him the match.

Those few extra seconds taken landing fish on the longer pole cost him the verdict.

Young John Kiely finished in third place with 2kg 631g which, compared to Eddie Coales' modest one kilo sandwiched between second and third did not really show the venue as being particularly fair. Nigel's final total of 1kg 443g put him well out of contention for the top honours and, because his section was split into two by the bridge, he did not stand much chance of winning that either. However, he did have at least 400g advantage over the anglers closest to him, and had at least asserted his superiority there.

The match had given me plenty to think about, not least the amount of hemp seed that Nigel had fed into his swim. His busy style with the pole was similar to Dickie Carr's in many respects. Several times, a slight lift of the pole to work the bloodworm bait resulted in a fish, that had given no indication on the float, being hooked. My technique was certainly lacking in this respect as I tended to wait for a positive indication before lifting into the bite. Obviously, this was sometimes too late.

August Bank Holiday Monday saw me awaiting my opportunity at the draw bag for a match pegged slightly above the Stretton length at Horninglow and Masefield. Again, on what was an apparently fair venue, there was a definite keenness to draw the higher numbered pegs on the Masefield section. Most of the favoured spots had gone by the time that I had my chance at the draw bag and I picked peg 14 on the Horninglow section.

As the match length is permanently pegged I was able to find out exactly where this draw would put me. First of all, I discovered that it had put me very close to Nigel as he had drawn peg 15! We were almost dead in the centre of the Horninglow section in an area of reed beds and far bank trees. The reed beds had rather sketchy

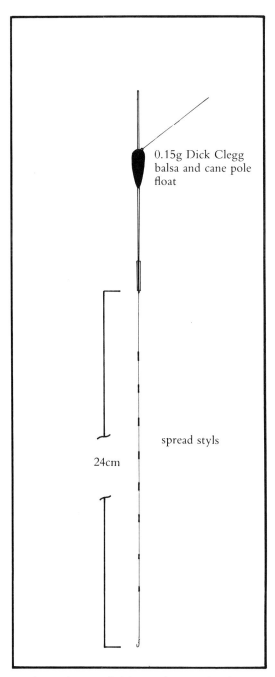

0.15g Dick Clegg balsa and cane pole float

spread styls

24cm

My long pole rig on the Trent and Mersey Canal at Horninglow.

carp form, whilst the trees towards Nigel's end of the reeds had produced decent chub from time to time.

As pre-match intelligence had suggested, my draw put me smack in the middle of the reeds, with an inviting indentation in them offering the fish some cover from boats. I have often found reeds to be a good fish-holding feature on canals, but Nigel lowered my spirits by saying that the area that we were in was too shallow to encourage many fish into the reeds. Plumbing the depth I discovered how right he had been. With only a couple of dozen centimetres of depth up against the reeds, it didn't look as though there would be many roach in the peg.

Nigel's swim was different altogether. He had the reed bed slightly to his left, a small bush opposite and overhanging trees downstream to his right. Although his peg was just as shallow I could see that he might be in with the chance of a bonus fish or two. I set up two rigs as Nigel had done on the previous match – one very short for the inside and one long pole for the main line of attack. I decided to follow Nigel as closely as possible so I fed in exactly the same amount of bait at the start of the match. I also decided to adopt his short line to start method, attempting to pick up a few gudgeon whilst the far bank groundbait settled.

Fifteen minutes flew by while I managed to catch just one gudgeon. Obviously the far bank had to be a better option so I decided to switch methods. Nigel was still fishing the short pole so, I guessed correctly, he was doing rather better on it than I had managed. Even on the long pole I was struggling to put fish together, and a troublesome wind meant that tackle control was very difficult. Although I was fishing quite a short line on the pre-prepared rig, the shallow nature of my peg meant that I had more line above the float

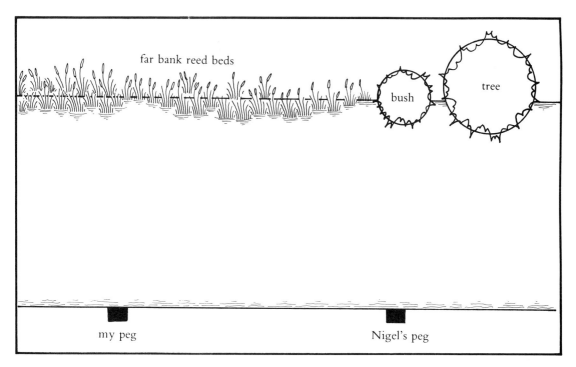

My and Nigel's pegs on the Trent and Mersey Canal at Horninglow.

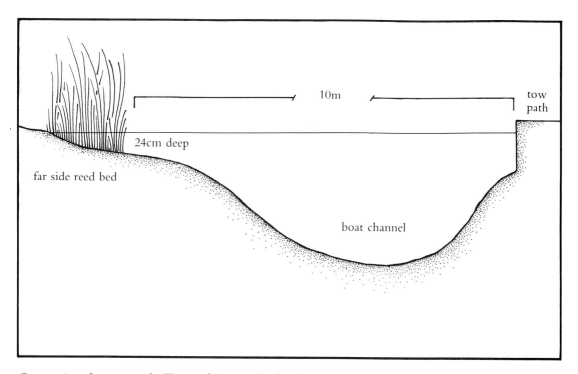

Cross-section of my peg on the Trent and Mersey Canal at Horninglow.

than was good for me. By removing nearly a metre of excess nylon I was able to improve my tackle control dramatically, and improve my catch rate.

Unfortunately, the average size of the fish that I was catching from the far bank didn't hold much promise of beating Nigel, who was doubtless catching fish of a similar size rather more quickly at shorter range. Almost on the hour, Nigel switched tactics, having taken forty or so fish on the near side line. I had about half that number. However, I was quite relieved when Nigel also struggled on the far bank, and although I could see no way of catching up with him numbers wise, at least the gap between us wasn't widening further.

Constant heavy boat traffic prevented the fish from settling on our groundbait, and by the half-way point of the match I was starting to give serious consideration

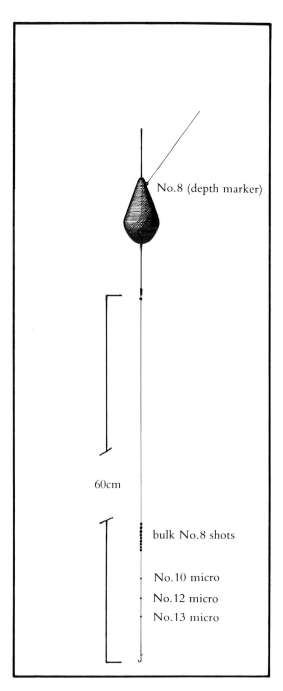

No.8 (depth marker)

60cm

bulk No.8 shots

No.10 micro

No.12 micro

No.13 micro

Very similar to the Milo Eris, and the best that I could do at short notice. I tackled my inside swim with a Milo Zeus float. I don't think that it was to blame for my not catching on the inside line!

My near side rig for the Trent and Mersey Canal at Horninglow. Note that the milo pole float is a slightly more bulbous pattern than Nigel's. It was the nearest that I could get.

to topping up the initial helping. Nigel must have had similar thoughts for he decided to introduce another large ball of feed. I rapidly followed suit and concentrated even harder, willing the bite rate to increase. Sadly, the great revival failed to happen, and both Nigel and myself continued to catch at a rather pedestrian rate.

The angler drawn on my left, on the peg running into the reeds decided that he had endured enough, packed and left. One less to worry about. Dense near side vegetation had meant that Nigel's catch rate on the short pole had been hidden from me. The long pole was a different matter though, and I could see that he was now coming back empty on the majority of occasions. I was still picking up odd fish and sensed that I might have an opportunity to catch up his early advantage.

Despite feeding it continuously, the hemp seed failed to attract a single bite. I decided that the boats were probably dispersing both fish and feed in my swim, and attempted to make something positive happen by repeating my opening helping of three tennis-ball-sized dollops of groundbait. Again my catch rate hardly altered but a few better samples were now falling to the bloodworm – only a score or so of grams; but better than the previous average and heartening all the same.

Just over an hour of the match remained and I was making inroads into Nigel's early advantage. Both his catch rate and activity seemed to have slowed down, which hinted that he might have abandoned the bloodworm hookbait in favour of something more attractive to bigger fish. This was dramatically confirmed when I saw him start to inch his pole slowly back across the canal, its internal elastic running out at full stretch towards the far bank.

By swapping to a caster instead of the bloodworm, and fishing tight to the small bush opposite, he had managed to hook a

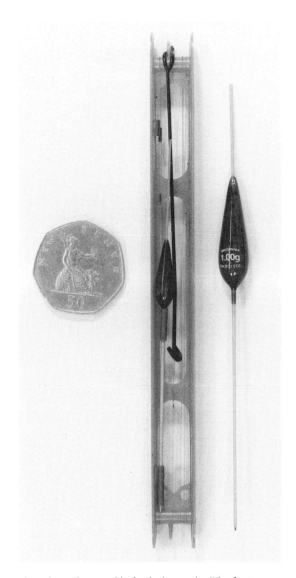

A ready-made-up tackle for the long pole. The float next to the winder illustrates the pattern, but greatly exaggerates the size. I have found this pattern to be a useful alternative during the winter.

good chub. With only a size 24 hook and 33g line the fish had to be handled with kid gloves, most of the rather dour struggle taking place in the boat channel, well out of harm's way. After what seemed like an eternity the chub was safely netted and, at close to a kilo and a half, it represented a hefty bonus on a fairly difficult day.

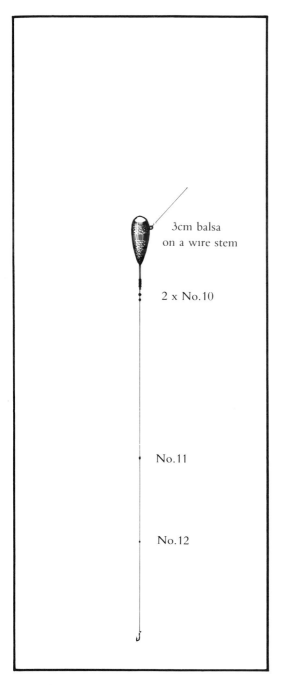

My preferred caster set-up for canals. But Nigel Bull just sticks one on to his bloodworm rig – and who am I to argue?

Although this one fish alone would probably make the difference between Nigel winning the match or finishing well down the list, he decided to stick to the caster in the hope of another decent chub which would undoubtedly seal the honours for him. I also decided that the caster might be worth a go, although my peg lacked many of the attractive features that might tempt a chub into it.

After fifteen minutes of inactivity Nigel started to run out of patience and mentioned that he was starting to think about swapping back to bloodworm. My view was that any time spent catching nothing at this late stage of the match was time wasted. I told him that if he lost the match by a few grams he might rue the decision to ignore a few more small fish that would almost certainly fall to the bloodworm. Nigel agreed with this thinking and picked up two or three more gudgeon on bloodworm before giving the caster yet another try.

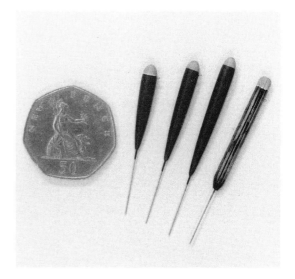

These are my choice for caster fishing on canals. Especially during the summer months when boat traffic causes the canal to flow due to the increased use of locks.

I had abandoned hope of catching a fish on caster and so switched back to blood-worm for what was left of the match, to see what might happen as much as anything. My bait supply was naturally low by this stage so I split my pack of hook blood-worms into the feed so that I at least had something to throw at the fish. Instead of a bombardment, I decided to feed small, soft balls of feed at frequent intervals. My catch rate increased immediately. If only I had tried this tactic sooner.

I had to be content with a final half-hour flurry, but the fish were coming quickly enough to suggest that, if the match had been extended by an hour, I might have been in with a chance of the minor honours. One problem, though, was my eagerness to put more fish into my net, which resulted in me missing a lot of bites by hitting them too soon. As is always the case in such situations, the final whistle came very swiftly and I weighed in a modest 623g. Nigel easily beat this with 1kg 925g which won him the match, but only by a margin of eight grams.

I was in the unique position of having suggested something that had given him the verdict. The few extra bloodworm fish had indeed proved their worth – something like £5 per gram on the day! On the other side of the coin, he had, he confessed, missed a bite on caster when his float was hidden by the small bush. He had felt the bite rather than seen it. Had he landed the culprit the match would have been his by an even bigger margin.

Like a great many anglers, Nigel is well aware of what is going on around him during the course of a match. He had noticed my increased catch rate towards the end of the match and was interested to know how I had achieved it. In retrospect, the little and often feed could have been a better method on the day, although the initial heavy feed would still have been a

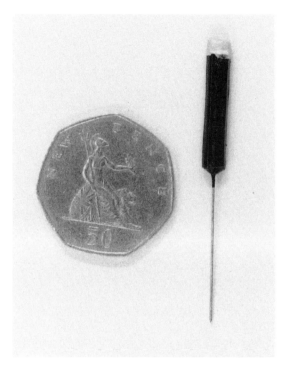

Another float for caster fishing, this time home-made. Obviously, it looks a bit cruder than the shop-bought floats, but, if it's good enough for Kevin Ashurst, it's good enough for me. The simple peacock quill with wire stem is a proven winner.

good ploy to concentrate the fish at the outset. The only drawback to this was that I had nowhere near enough feed to have kept the swim going in that fashion for the duration of the match.

I had noticed that Nigel had not been so busy pole-wise as in the match at Stretton. This, he said, was due to the extreme shallowness of the swim. The fish had to be given a little longer to take the bait than in a deeper swim where there is a natural delay between the fish taking the bite and a bite registering. Had I known that, my finale would have been even more produc-tive. Looking at Nigel's catch at the weigh-in, it crossed my mind that our catches were very similar, apart from the big chub, and on small fish alone I might just have

Just to show that I can catch on a short pole! Typically not in a match situation! What you can't see in this photograph is that the swim was seething with bubbles after only two small balls of groundbait.

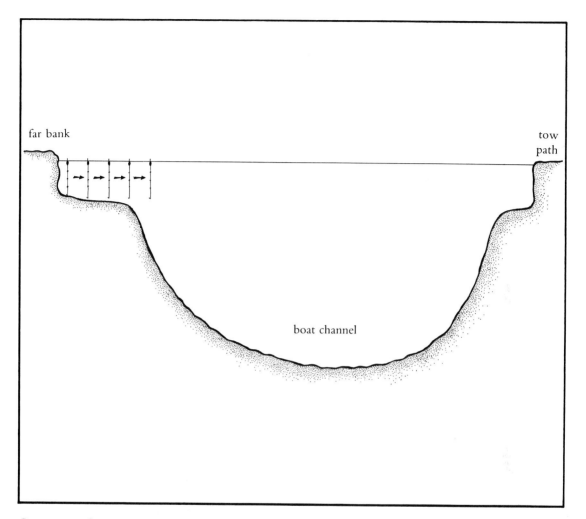

far bank

tow path

boat channel

Cross-section of canal, showing Nigel Bull's dragging off the far shelf technique – deadly for roach in autumn when boat traffic subsides.

beaten him. However, there are a couple of factors that bear consideration.

I had fished the long pole for more of the match and Nigel had fished on a far less productive bait for the best part of an hour. Having said that, my few better fish at the end might have been vital. I had no answer to his bonus chub though! Tackle-wise, our terminal set-ups had been very similar, although I obviously had the advantage of the close scrutiny of Nigel's gear during the Stretton match.

My lack of fish on the short line disturbed me though, and Nigel was curious to know exactly how far out I had fished, in case I had gone too far! I explained that I couldn't have fished any tighter unless I had turned my box around to face the opposite direction. On that subject I had to console myself with the thought that Nigel had failed to catch at close range in the Stretton match a few days earlier.

Perhaps groundbait accuracy (or the lack of it), cost me dearly when I drew next to Nigel Bull.

Nigel's far bank method appeared to be quite simple. However, that was mainly due to his proficiency in it. Also, Nigel did mention that I hadn't really seen him at his best, with autumn a far better time to see the long pole at work. With fewer boats on the canal, the roach are more inclined to drop down off the far shelf, which means that the angler is not tied to that very shallow area. However, the chances are that the main feed will still be introduced on to the shelf, as close to the drop off point as possible, capturing the attention of roach in both areas. By drawing back the pole tackle, the angler can also offer his bait slightly off bottom over the deepening water which should, all things being equal, catch him more roach than gudgeon. Simple in theory, but I think that it might take me quite a bit of practice to become competent in this refinement. Nigel did stress that practice was the key to his mastery of that technique, simply because it gave a good idea of what was going on below the surface.

I did feel that I was showing some improvement on that subject. During the match, I had been considering topping up the far bank feed when Nigel confirmed my suspicions by doing so. However, it would be wrong to suggest that Nigel's canal success is based only on one method, and a thorough knowledge of a wide variety of methods is required for consistent results. Although not in favour of bait bans, Nigel certainly wasn't averse to visiting canal venues where bloodworm was banned, and had enjoyed good results on them. The methods that he used under those conditions would more than fill another book!

3　Dickie Carr

Dickie Carr was the first Southern angler to be invited to join the England World Championship squad when it was run by Stan Smith, a fact which guaranteed his reputation, as at that time the Southern match scene was still trying to escape from its reputation as an inferior cousin to the Midland and Northern scene.

Size limit and roving matches had long been the bane of serious Southern anglers, although the former did have a part in establishing some of their most successful anglers as bleak catchers *par excellence*. Unfortunately it also type-cast them as being obsessed with pole fishing, at a time when English matchmen, as a whole, were only too willing to concede the superiority of the continentals as far as pole techniques were concerned.

In some circles, Dickie was regarded as a token Southerner in the England squad, although his performances in open matches around the country tended to belie this. What was clear was that, at that time, Dickie was one of the few Southern anglers to take notice of how Midland and Northern match anglers went about their business, and he applied their tactics to his home venues with devastating effect. A major influence on him, in those days, was Ivan Marks, a great natural angler and one whom Dickie greatly admires. Dickie's success on Southern bream venues was in no small way due to Ivan's influence, though Ivan must also have learned quite a lot from the Southern ace.

As I mentioned earlier, pole fishing has always enjoyed a lot of popularity in the south, and naturally Dickie had to be conversant with these techniques to compete on some of the venues where the pole was a necessity. Not surprisingly, the current boom in pole fishing nationwide has seen him leap to even greater prominence. However, it was one venue in particular that saw Dickie's name repeatedly in the news – the River Lea.

The Lea is certainly not a venue for the faint-hearted for, even at its best, it is unpredictable and some of its match lengths are notoriously difficult. I well remember a series of joke articles about the river at a fictional venue called 'Gruellers End' – a name which did not inspire confidence. However, it does have a fair variety of fishing along its length, with quite a few different techniques required for consistent results. Dickie's match record on the River Lea shows, if nothing else, his mastery of a wide range of methods – from waggler fishing for chub to pole fishing for bleak. He wins on them all.

Perhaps the hardest part of this piece was actually catching up with Dickie Carr in the first place. Early season usually sees him still engaged in Irish Festival fishing (another aspect of his angling success), whilst this season (1988), he had other urgent matters to attend to. With the World Championships set for what looked to be a pole venue, Dickie was again on International standby having performed well in some of the England trials. He was also engaged in the British Pole Championship, winning the first round very early in the season.

The 44-year-old bait and tackle wholesaler was also enjoying one of his most profitable seasons business-wise, and sheer pressure of work in one of angling's boom summers, left him fewer hours on the waterside. However, I was at last able to catch up with Dickie on one of a series of evening matches on the River Lea at Cooks Ferry, a less than prepossessing venue. The match length there runs through an industrial estate – a setting far removed from angling's pastoral roots, and one which I found grim indeed.

Nevertheless, the matches find no shortage of takers, and tend to attract a very high-class field. Best known amongst the hopefuls were the Trevs Browning anglers, led by Dave Vincent, who, like Dickie, had been performing well in the England trials. But on the whole, the matches seemed to be attended by any London-based angler with aspirations of competing at the highest level.

Most species of fish are present along the Cooks Ferry length, with roach, dace and skimmers the most prominent. Accordingly, methods which will be successful with these species are favoured, especially those techniques that have potential for catching all three. One of the reasons for this is the short duration of evening matches. These short sprints leave little room for experimentation and anglers need fairly instant results to ensure that they keep in touch. They also need to avoid blank spells, if possible, as once off the pace they may only get back by taking a calculated gamble.

Even though the matches are short, the anglers are still keen to pace their swims correctly, aiming to catch fish from start to finish rather than in a short burst. This can entail a possible back-up plan in the event of one method dying on them, although

this is not the only eventuality when such a ploy may be turned to. It may be that an angler will switch methods in an attempt to prolong his catching spell by resting his swim, or it could be a calculated change to a 'sleeping' method that is designed to attract a larger stamp of fish late in the match in an attempt to pull away from the field.

My only previous experience on the River Lea had been some ten years earlier when I had drawn a very poor section in the Lea Championships. I was drawn opposite an old pumping station and was told that that particular swim had a very sketchy history of reasonable weights. In fact, only one reasonable weight had come from the area, and that seemed to have been a long time ago from what I was told.

Unusually for those days, I had taken some bloodworm along to the match but these, fished on an eight-metre glass-fibre pole, only attracted sticklebacks and a few see-through gudgeon that were never going to be enough to get me into the prizes. I did manage to catch one or two tiny chub and roach on the waggler – a method that I was much more confident with – but even these were no better in real terms. I finished the match with around half a kilo of bits and pieces – not bad for the section but nowhere in the match. Most of the weights in the area which beat me consisted of single, big chub. It seemed to me that a venue where success depended on how well fed the one fish that you landed was did not have a lot to offer.

However, I was keen to see what Dickie made of the venue as I thought that lessons learned on hard waters such as the Lea could only stand me in good stead on the more prolific venues close to home. Dickie's working hours meant that we only just arrived in time for the draw, and my first view of the wind-whipped match length filled me with trepidation. Another reason for Dickie's late arrival was his requirement of fresh bait, in this case bloodworm and joker, which he had scraped himself (a task he enjoys almost as much as going fishing).

The turbulent venue certainly didn't put Dickie off, and he was even more pleased when he drew peg 17 which put him in an area that he fancied, although he thought that the lower teens were better. Nevertheless, he thought that his peg offered him the chance of catching the couple of kilos normally needed to get into the money, with an outside chance of winning the match. Looking along the match length, it seemed that some of the areas that Dickie didn't fancy had rather more to offer. A wide section close to the draw looked favourite to hold a few skimmers, which Dickie agreed with. However, he said that the wide swims were very unpredictable, which, for a venue like the Lea, must mean that they can be heartbreakers.

To my untutored eye the Lea looked very similar to a Midlands canal, but on a slightly larger scale, even to the extent of having similar proportions and features. As I thought this, I noticed a boat travelling down the river, making the scene look quite familiar. The sluggish flow meant that the wind would play havoc with bait presentation, and I was keen to find out how Dickie intended to master the conditions. I was also interested to find out what he thought his catch would be made up of, and what method he was going to use to achieve it.

First, though, I asked Dickie about the bleak prospect on the match length, as I had heard that Cooks Ferry was one of the better venues for the species. It transpired that these fish only come into their own during the winter months when the river is carrying extra colour, although Dickie said that not too many matches were fished under those conditions as it gave the bleak experts too much of an advantage. He was a little saddened by this as he had made use of his frequent trips to the continent to pick up some bleak fishing tips from the Italians, with the result that he now felt a good few paces ahead of the chasing pack.

The only advantage that I could see Cooks Ferry offering as a match venue was that it was possible to drive right up to the pegs. Once settled, the constant roar of heavy traffic turned fishing into an acoustic nightmare. The two most favoured methods on the Lea at Cooks Ferry were pole and waggler, with the former a majority choice by a vast margin. Apparently, the waggler was only gaining in popularity on the strength of a recent win on the venue. Dickie had decided to stick with the pole, in spite of drawing a peg that looked to have real waggler possibilities. A tempting looking bush opposite hinted at a chub or two although these would obviously be a gamble. With only three hours at his disposal, Dickie decided that the gamble was not justified. A five-hour match would have been different though, and the waggler would undoubtedly have been brought into play at some stage.

One of the first things that I noticed was Dickie's choice of pole – an Italian Triana. It was not the lightest pole that I have ever handled, and certainly not in the same league as Sammy Mann's Maver Litium but it was one of the stiffest poles that I had examined. Dickie told me that he was not too worried about the weight of a pole (within reason) so long as the action was right. He also pointed out that the Triana was a good work-horse pole, usable on big-weight venues whereas some lighter but flimsier poles were not. He also confessed to being very hard on poles and had experienced a few less substantial models giving up on him. Another point of interest was his revelation that a new Triana pole with his name on it was going to be

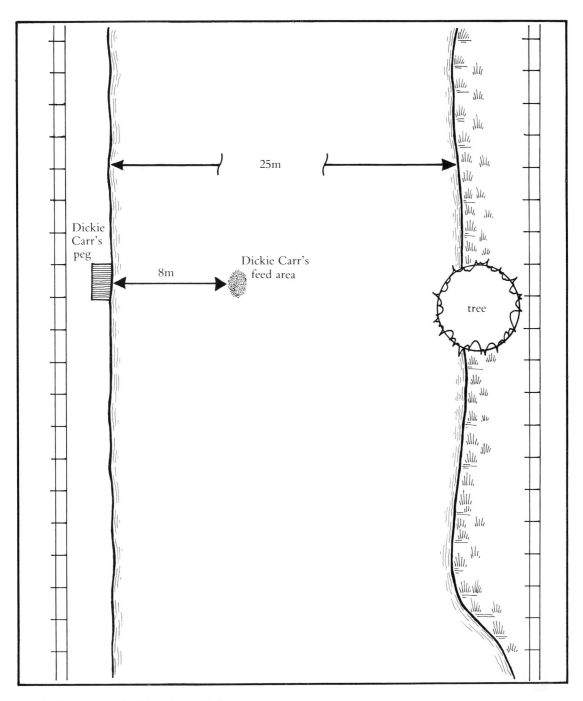

25m

Dickie
Carr's
peg

Dickie Carr's
feed area

8m

tree

Dickie Carr's peg on the River Lea at Cooks Ferry.

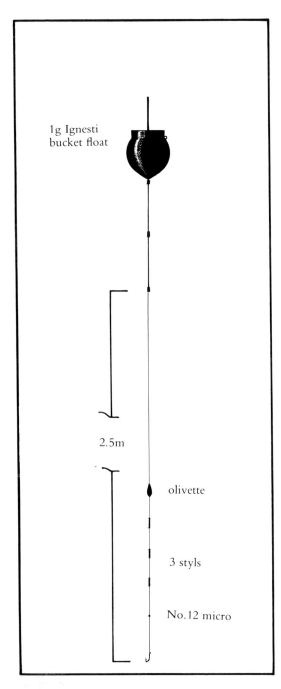

1g Ignesti
bucket float

2.5m

olivette

3 styls

No.12 micro

Dickie Carr's rig for the River Lea at Cooks Ferry.

imported. It would be lighter than the current model without too much sacrifice of strength.

Because of the strong wind, and the possibility of more tow on the water, Dickie opted for an unusually shaped Ignesti float which, in his words, reminded him of a bucket. However, he said that the float was one of the most stable patterns that he had come across and, with a 1-gram capacity, it offered great advantages of control over more slender floats with lighter shotting. The shotting of the float was simplicity itself, a tungsten olivette at around thirty centimetres from the hook, with only a couple of droppers below. I noticed that Dickie used very short hook-links on his pole set-ups and he explained the reasoning behind this. When using very fine hooklinks he did not like to have shot on them in case the line was weakened further. I had come to the same conclusion some time ago with regard to some of my canal tackles, and it was nice to know that I might be thinking in the right direction.

A size 22 hook to 0.35kg line hinted that bloodworm was to be Dickie's first choice of bait, a correct assumption as I subsequently found out. Plumbing the depth took quite some time, and Dickie found about two and a half metres on the line that he was most interested in fishing. However, he continued to plumb around the swim for some time to familiarise himself with its contours. He was also looking for tackle stealing snags which would disrupt his catching pattern. He did not want to drop a load of groundbait into a spot, only to find that it was virtually unfishable due to snags.

Having made a similar mistake on a local canal a couple of years previously I understood his caution. The experience had certainly done me some good in retrospect. Nothing much in the way of snags revealed itself and now Dickie was able to make the final adjustments to his terminal tackle. This comprised of shortening the free line between pole tip and float in order to retain exact control in the windy conditions. Actually the original line length did not look too unmanageable but Dickie was keen to get his presentation as near perfect as was possible.

Although the rig had been ready-made up on a winder, the final testing came on the bankside. Removing the plummet, Dickie tried a few runs through the swim without bait on the hook to test the shotting of the float. I noticed that it was shotted far lower in the water than seemed normal with pole floats, only the merest fraction of bristle protruding above the surface. I thought that he had perhaps overshotted the float, but was told that this was his normal preference. Dotting down the bristle means that the angler has to keep lifting the float very slightly in order to be able to see it. This imparts movement to the baited hook which often attracts a bite.

Dickie felt that this working of the bait was integral to success and shotted his floats so that he had little option but to do it. On this occasion, though, he thought that the float might have been dotted a little too low, with the wind-driven wave action submerging the float for long periods. However, he did not react as I expected, and remove a shot; instead he smeared the bristle of his float with Vaseline, which made it just buoyant enough to have the correct amount of show. Something else that I hadn't thought of.

With a few minutes remaining before the start of the match Dickie mixed up the groundbait that he hoped would last for its duration. The make-up of his mix was fairly simple – 90 per cent Van Den Eynde Secret and 10 per cent brown bread crumb. No leam was used as Dickie felt that this attracted too many small fish. I would have thought the exact opposite!

The groundbait was intended to carry a litre of raw jokers which Dickie had freshly scraped. Hopefully the six balls of feed that he intended to introduce would keep the fish interested all match. In readiness for the starting whistle, Dickie formed up half a dozen tennis-ball-sized helpings, treating three of them to slow down their break-up time once in the water. This was achieved by simply glazing the balls by squeezing them with wet hands, the old bream anglers' trick to enable groundbait to be thrown a good distance in one piece. Apparently it worked under water too.

On the starting signal, Dickie lowered his pole float into position and used it as a marker for his groundbait. This he dropped just short of the target in order that he would be sure to be fishing on top of his feed and not a good way inside of it. The results of the initial feed were not long in coming. Tiny, almost transparent roach, gudgeon and ruffe showed that the jokers were encouraging fish to feed. However, Dickie was also loose feeding casters into his swim, on exactly the same line as the joker groundbait. I had never seen this technique before, but was assured by Dickie that casters and bloodworm were perfectly compatible baits.

The bites were easy to see, even in the windy conditions and Dickie wasn't missing many. However, the average size of fish was very small, and it was obvious that he would have to work very hard to put together a winning catch of fish in the ten gram range. On the next peg upstream, the angler was catching a better stamp of fish and had opened up a substantial lead, the angler upstream of him, fishing the waggler, had hooked and lost a carp.

By the end of the first hour, the bankside grapevine revealed that Dickie was losing touch with the leaders – his fish simply were not big enough. So, earlier than he would have liked, and mainly for investigative purposes, Dickie chanced a drop in with a caster on the hook. Encouragingly, this resulted in him catching a roach of some 150g – much nearer to the size that he wanted. In order to assess the method's potential, and to see if it was a fluke capture, Dickie tried another put in with the caster. This time the float cocked and kept on going and a roach of around twice the size of the first caster fish found itself being persuaded towards the waiting landing net. Unfortunately, the hook pulled out at the last moment leaving Dickie annoyed that he had not changed up from the tiny size 22. At least it proved that there were fish there and feeding, so he decided to see just how many he could winkle out on the caster if he fished for them properly.

A size 18 hook was substituted and the float deepened off by a few centimetres in the style that he had found most effective for the caster. Now, though, the bites were very timid and he had great difficulty in hitting them. Obviously the lost fish had unsettled the shoal even though it had been lost quite some distance away from them. With half of the match now gone, Dickie felt compelled to stick it out on the caster in the hope of better fish, but gradually the bites dried up completely and he decided to switch back to bloodworm in the hope of catching a fish, however small.

For some reason, this ploy also failed, although the angler on the next peg upstream had been catching on the method throughout. Then, out of the blue, Dickie at last attracted a bite on the bloodworm tackle. A routine lift of the pole saw elastic pulled steadily from the tip as what looked to be a snag fouled the line. Increasing the tension slightly in an effort to spring the hook free resulted in the snag shifting position and trundling slowly and unstoppably upstream. Dickie swiftly added sections to his pole to follow the beast's progress but unfortunately ran out of sec-

tions before it ran out of steam and broke the frail hooklink. Now it was obvious why Dickie's swim had died.

The passage of what appeared to be another carp through the upstream angler's peg stopped him from catching for a while. The smaller fish did not seem to like the company of the big fellows. Not surprisingly, the small fish now returned on Dickie's bloodworm line, and although he caught them rapidly during the last part of the match he said that they had come back too late. As a last ditch attempt, Dickie doubled up his bloodworm on the hook trying to pick up a skimmer or two. Even this was thwarted as he caught ruffe instead, albeit of a bigger size than he had been catching on the single bait.

The scales told a sorry story at the end of the match as Dickie weighed in just less than a kilo, not in with any chance of a prize. However, the one fish that he lost would probably have given him victory by a comfortable margin, and who knows what he might have caught had the big fish not been frightening off the smaller ones. Dickie accepted all of this with good grace. After all, losing is all part of match fishing. Though I could think of a few anglers who would have been tearing their hair out if faced with that situation.

Dickie's temperament was absolutely faultless, especially as he had a lot of good-natured ribbing to endure after recording one of the lower totals weighed in. Unfortunately, a few months elapsed before I met up with Dickie again, although he had been very busy in the meantime. A fortnight's trip to Ireland and further pre-booked matches at home meant that he had very little time to spare. He also managed to get through to the final of the British Pole Championships on the Gloucester Canal, taking the title with a fine performance. The poor result on River Lea at Cooks Ferry was now a distant memory.

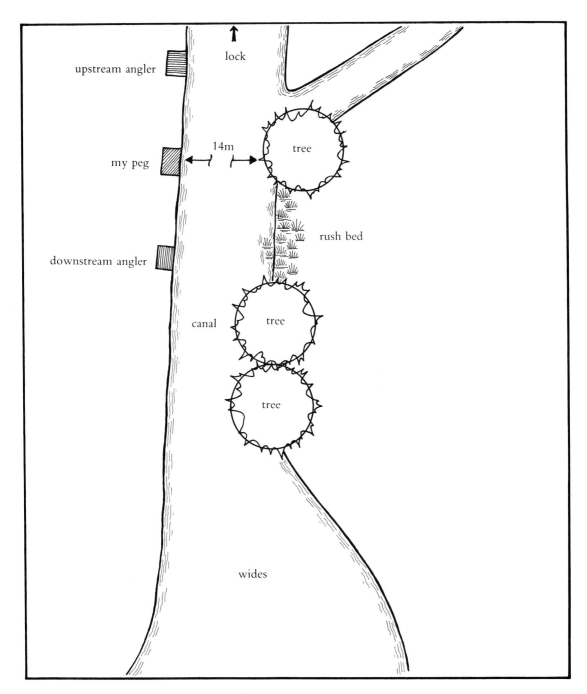

My peg at Kings Langley (Grand Union Canal).

Our next meeting was on the Grand Union Canal at Kings Langley – one of the nicest looking canal venues that I have seen and far easier on the eye than the River Lea. Bloodworm was banned on this match but that was unlikely to affect the outcome as the match was almost certain to be dominated by chub, with catches into double figures expected. The area that most anglers wanted to draw was the wides. At least nobody pretends that this canal is an even venue. Dickie told me that in around five visits he had drawn the wides once, winning the match with a catch of chub on the swimfeeder. This time he was not so lucky, and again faced a day of trying to make something out of nothing.

My draw was far different, as I pulled peg 79 from the bag – a noted flier which had produced match winning catches previously. Peg 79 was not on the wides but just upstream, almost opposite the point where a river entered the canal. Dickie told me that I would catch chub on maggot using the pole or a straight ledger. Nice and simple, I thought, and went off to see what my swim looked like. I found that it was exactly as described – a large tree overhanging opposite and looking very fishy indeed. The only problem was that the canal was still a little too wide for my eleven-metre Maestro pole to reach. A fourteen-metre pole would have been ideal. However, I fancied that I might be able to draw a few chub out from under the tree by steady feeding.

The next peg downstream was rather narrower, a comfortable eleven-metre reach, with reeds opposite and overhanging trees at the downstream end. However, the incoming stream, which I was told was carrying a little extra water, was causing a back current which meant that the canal was flowing back towards me on the opposite bank. Upstream, the angler could cast down to my tree, which meant that I might

have to share my fish with him, although as we tackled up, a good sized chub rolled in the lock cutting immediately to that angler's left, so I felt that he might not be bothering me too much after all.

I decided to set up the eleven-metre pole with the usual shortish line, and also a lead rod in case I had to go tight to the tree. Plumbing the depth, I found that I had a good metre of water as far across as I could fish the pole. Hopefully it would be stuffed full of suicidal chub. Immediately the whistle sounded to start the match, the angler on the upstream side of me made his intentions clear by casting as close as possible to the tree opposite my peg. Obviously I would have to share any chub that happened to be living under the tree, also, as we were both attempting to feed the swim and draw fish out to our area of operation, they would certainly not be going short of food.

I wasn't really happy with the way the pole was fishing. The main problem was getting the terminal tackle close enough to the tree. Accordingly, after only two or three puts in, I decided to change tactics and fish a straight ledger in similar fashion to the angler upstream. My downstream neighbour was also ledgering, straight across at the reeds, so we would soon have an idea of whether the method was going to work or not. We were all plagued by minnows as soon as the bait hit the water, and the tip was never still as they fought and fussed over the bait. I tried a couple of redworms on the hook in the hope that it might lessen the problem, but the minnows seemed determined to consume anything edible no matter now big.

I soon decided that a mini swimfeeder might provide an answer to the problem and, because it would put some bait near to the hook, might increase the chance of a chub. Though for some undefinable reason, I did not feel at all confident about catching

This is the small block-end swimfeeder that I used on the Grand Union Canal at Kings Langley. Perhaps I should have used a bigger one.

chub from the swim. I had the feeling that I was going to be in for a frustrating day.

The first hour of the match flew by. I discovered that the closer to the tree the feeder was cast, the more chance there was of losing the hooklink in an underwater snag. Obviously any chub that I hooked would be a bit of a handful. However, I was set up with a size 18 forged hook and 0.80kg hooklink (rather heavier than normal canal gear). Still the minnows were bothersome, and attempts to feed them off were a waste of time. I catapulted hemp into the swim in increasing amounts, in the hope that it might bring the chub on to the feed, and topped up the swimfeeders' helpings with regular pouchfuls of maggots.

Downstream of me the angler on the reed bed had switched methods and was now fishing the eleven-metre pole a metre or so short of the far side. Minnows were still giving him problems on this method, though by now we were both picking up an odd gudgeon or two as well. Hardly

match winning form. With about ninety minutes of the match gone, all three of us were fairly evenly matched. However, the downstream angler seemed to have spoiled things when he lifted into what was obviously a reasonable chub. Unfortunately for him it threw the hook just as he looked to be bringing it under control. I decided to stay with the swimfeeder in the short term as I didn't feel that I could reach the required distance on the eleven-metre pole.

However, he was into another chub within about five minutes of losing the first, landing this one and going about half a kilo into the lead of our three-peg battle. I decided that perhaps the pole did have some magic after all and swung it into action. Hardly had my tackle hit the water than the angler downstream was having his elastic stretched by yet another hefty chub. Obviously, he had a shoal on the go. Unfortunately this fish made itself fast in the far side reed bed and could not be persuaded to come out.

With all the turmoil caused by losing fish I felt sure that a chub might soon come my way. In retrospect though they probably did the opposite and melted back under the bushes to the downstream angler's right, further away from me. Still I had to be content with minnows and odd gudgeon, with the pole a real liability under the circumstances, as the bait was scarcely in the water long enough to attract a chub. Similarly afflicted was the angler upstream of me. He clearly thought that the tree was the holding spot and repeatedly cast his ledger/swimfeeder as close to its upstream edge as possible, without appreciable reward.

The angler downstream was now going for glory and determined not to lose any more chub. He was fishing 1.2kg line direct to a size 14 forged hook. Obviously this attracted fewer bites, but he still managed to nab another brace of chub in the

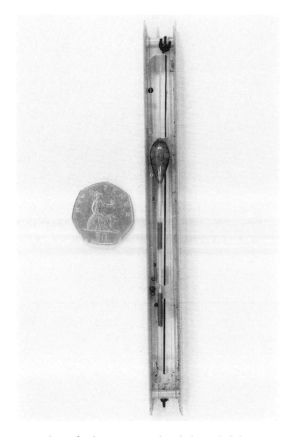

My pole rig for the Kings Langley chub. A slightly larger float than normal to cope with the flow.

Home-made canal floats for use with rod and line. Actually I didn't set up a running line for the Grand Union match. Why?

next hour. With a couple of hours left, he was clearly winning our little battle. I abandoned the pole, as one of the Maestro's shortcomings at eleven metres full stretch was making itself apparent – it was very heavy! The swimfeeder still achieved only minnows and gudgeon but at least it wasn't such an arm-aching prospect and it allowed me the opportunity of assembling a three-metre gudgeon rig. Really it was only a case of unravelling the ready-made winder and I was ready to go.

As chub were so obviously dominating this match, the change to small fish at this late stage of the match probably seems a

little crazy. However, I realised that there were a few gudgeon to be caught as I had been picking them up fairly quickly on the long pole and double maggot. If similar numbers were shoaled up close in there was a possibility of two to three kilos of them in what remained of the match. Although there would be some big weights on this match, two or three kilos is always a respectable weight on a canal and, as I was in an area where a good few of the individual prize winners would come from, I was in with a chance of sneaking the section by a process of elimination.

As I expected, there was a fair depth of

water on the three-metre line so I mixed the groundbait quite heavily. The flow from the stream opposite meant that all of the main pull was coming right back into my bank. It also meant that any snags would be deposited in that area as I soon found out to my cost. Although I did catch gudgeon on the inside line, I also suffered from repeated snag-ups. The gudgeon were a reasonable stamp at around eighty to the kilo but they were not coming quickly enough for me to reach the three kilos that I felt I would need to be in with a chance of a section pick-up. In some ways I was rather relieved, for I would have hated to have wasted so much of the match chasing shadows, with the potential of a five-kilo gudgeon catch from a full five hours' effort, right under my nose. So, after that fifteen-minute respite, it was back to the far bank and another go on the eleven-metre pole. With an hour left, the angler downstream of me had another spell of frantic action when he hooked a carp. He was determined to land it and the carp was equally determined that it would have its freedom. As is so often the way, the carp presented the better argument.

A carelessly driven narrowboat (one of the few that we saw), gave me a brief hope of a chub or two as it ploughed straight through my downstream neighbour's peg. I felt sure that it would have flushed some chub before it and they would have found refuge under my tree. At least I was correct in this assumption, but unfortunately the chub ran too far and the angler upstream of me nabbed one on the straight ledger. I began to feel that it was not my day.

With only a few minutes of the match remaining the downstream angler decided to fine down again to a size 18 to 0.80kg line and was instantly rewarded with another chub. I couldn't help thinking that I would have been back on that tackle rather sooner if I had been in the same

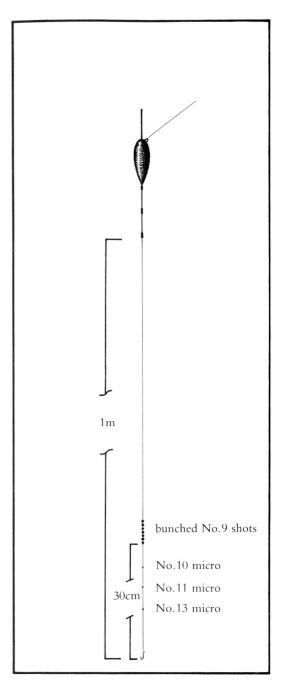

0.50m milo pole float, used briefly on the Grand Union Canal at Kings Langley.

Milo Apollo float. I set up a rig with one of these on the Grand Union Canal. I decided that the turbulent swim required bossing with a float that offered some stability.

position. A biteless hour is a long time when there are obviously a few fish in the peg. However, he had the last laugh at the weigh-in with a level three kilos. I had just short of a kilo and so didn't bother to weigh in. I had, in fact, caught a chub with five minutes to go in the match, but at a mind-boggling 10 centimetres long, it didn't boost my weight by any appreciable amount.

The angler upstream of me did decide to weigh in on the strength of the chub that he had landed. However, while his back was turned, it executed what is apparently quite a well known party trick of the Grand Union chub and jumped out of his keep-net. The match winner, not surprisingly, came from the wides – Middy 279's Sid Best, making it a hat trick on the venue. After the match he came along and had a look at my peg and told me that he had

won an earlier match off it. That day he had fished only a ten-metre pole but with quite a long line, to land five chub for six kilos. In retrospect, I should have tried the longer line but it is easy to be wise after the event.

Sid also mentioned that the canal seemed to be pulling more strongly than when he had drawn the swim, and that might have made quite a difference. He also mentioned that the peg on the reed bed was far more consistent in producing chub even though it seldom coughed up enough to win. Dickie had a tough day as he suspected he might at the outset. However, he had caught a kilo and a half of gudgeon in the last couple of hours after not fishing for them in the earlier part of the match. He felt that he had made a mistake by not going for them from the start as the swim obviously had potential for that species. He had fallen into the trap of fishing for species that were not there – a mistake that he would not repeat on that venue.

One thought that did cross my mind after the match was that both myself and Dickie would have done rather better if we had been drawn on each other's pegs! Dickie thought that this was fair comment, although he thought that the chub might not have been particularly evident in my peg as I had not caught a decent one. It would have been reasonable to expect at least one fish just for turning up. Had I caught just one or two decent chub then I really would have felt that I had made a mistake somewhere along the line. As I did not catch any I felt a little better about it. Perhaps there weren't any there on the day.

One of the match organisers also made me feel a little better about blowing a flier. He told me that a couple of seasons previously I would have been in with an outstanding chance. Now the noted pegs on the venue (and it is a day-ticket water) get a lot of hammer and don't produce as regularly as was once the case. The boom peg was another one that he cited as being overfished and nothing like the peg that it once was. Having said that, I had drawn one of the best pegs on the length and had not even managed a section pick-up from it. If I learned nothing else it was that the top anglers never have that sort of thing happen to them. If they draw a good peg then they win; end of story.

4 Sammy Mann

There is one major area where I disagree with what the late Clive Smith had to say about match angling, and that is with regard to team fishing or, more specifically, team anglers. Team anglers, as such, did not exist for Clive. He had great anglers in his teams, but the term 'team angler' was not part of his vocabulary. He said that good team anglers needed to be successful on the open circuit to have the edge that would ensure that they got ten kilos from a ten-kilo peg, not seven or eight kilos.

However, in saying that I believe that he did some brilliant team anglers a grave disservice. Some anglers do turn to team fishing because of ill fortune at the draw bag. The law of averages does not work in angling (well, perhaps it does but it can be over a very long period rather than season by season), and a poor peg in a team environment still has to be fished as hard as a flier. In an open match, the angler can pack up and go home or go and watch someone else, or he can stick it out, but rarely will an angler win anything off a poor peg, especially if his luck is out.

If a team angler draws a poor peg then he still has a job to do for the team, for it will stand or fall on the results of the poorest pegs rather than the best ones, and at least the angler can gain some justification for wasting his day perhaps catching very little. There are quite a few successful open circuit anglers who are just not used to struggling for a bite, and in these situations the team angler comes into his own. Sometimes the tactics that will catch an angler

ten kilos will prevent him from catching two kilos when that might be the best that he can expect from the swim. Not only that, but some anglers who are used to catching plenty of fish run out of ideas when they are faced with a situation where they can't.

Very often, the good team anglers remain the unsung heroes, their third or fourth in section from a worthless peg often overshadowed by the section winners and the anglers who manage to make the main prize list, but their worth is inestimable. More so because they tend to be more dependable than some of the mercurial talents. They consistently come up with the goods.

However, as I said earlier, the law of averages may at last begin to work, and an angler otherwise known as a steady team man will have his chance of glory. The nice thing about when these anglers do start to do well in individual matches is that *everyone* is pleased, which in the cynical world of match angling is something rather special. Perhaps the reasons are two fold – the consistent winners know that there but for the grace of God go they, and the other hopefuls have their optimism rekindled. It is human nature to cheer for the underdog.

Sammy Mann is one of those anglers who by sheer hard work built themselves a formidable reputation as a team angler. For a good many years he was an ever-present and dependable member of the successful Starlets team, sharing in their many triumphs. However, a recent switch to

Sammy Mann, a superb team angler now reaping the individual rewards.

Keenets Aquarians resulted in a timely change of fortune, on the individual front, for one of the most popular anglers on the open circuit. A string of good results in 1987 on a variety of venues was a mere forerunner of what was to come this term, for by the time that I caught up with Sammy, in late October, he had already picked up money in twenty-three matches – an excellent striking rate. His most notable success came in the John Smiths team championships on the River Avon, where he swung the balance for the Keenets Aquarians team by taking the top weight on the day – a popular result in every sense.

Although an adaptable angler, Sammy considers himself a running water specialist, at home on venues such as the Severn and Trent. However, the Warwickshire Avon is his favourite venue, and has been the scene of many triumphs. For some years, Sammy has kept a caravan on a permanent site at Hampton Ferry – a pleasant weekend retreat and an ideal starting point for matches in the area. It also gives him ample opportunity to keep in touch with the venue (vital to success on the Avon as the slightest change in the seasons can see different methods taking over). The angler that wishes to keep on top must be able to anticipate these changes, something that Sammy is getting down to a fine art. Any slight alterations brought about by flood or low water can be monitored, as well as the effects that they have on the distribution of the fish population. Again, Sammy is well placed to be in on the action.

Some years ago, Gladding began a trend by organising an invitation open match on Evesham town water. Spectators flocked to the event and it was a great success. Around that time, a series of Wednesday Open matches was organised on the Hampton Ferry section just downstream. For some reason, these really caught the attention of the angling media and the results and match run-downs were always published. It quickly became evident that this area of the Avon was the place to go if you wanted to build an angling reputation by competing against the big boys.

My first view of the river must have been around fifteen years ago at one of these Wednesday Opens, at a time when Max Winters was having a phenomenal run of success. I travelled down to watch with a group of anglers from Leicester which included Ivan Marks, Stan Piecha and Stu Killen. The river was very cold and bites were hard to come by but I had never seen such an array of angling talent in one place before.

If my memory serves me correctly, Clive Smith won the match with about seven kilos, fishing waggler and casters from a peg near to the pump at Hampton Ferry. Alan Higgs, I believe, took second, I think from the next peg. What a performance those two put on, taking 90 per cent of their catch in the last hour. They made fishing the Avon look remarkably easy. I cannot think of many of the great anglers who have not made their mark at Hampton Ferry and Evesham, and the fact that it seemed to be held in high regard as an angler's water made it a bench-mark by which ability was judged.

To some extent, this is still true today, and no matter how tetchily the river is fishing (it can be a very fickle venue), there is seldom any shortage of anglers willing to have a go. For some reason the venue tends to lend itself to spectators. The fish seem more tolerant of bankside activity than on some other venues, although they are very choosey about the way in which bait must be presented. Winning is nice anywhere, the Avon included. To win at Evesham and Hampton Ferry tends to be just that bit more special – the equivalent of a National Hunt trainer getting a winner at the Cheltenham Festival – the prestige is enormous.

Sammy Mann on peg 139 at Hampton Ferry on the Warwickshire Avon, opposite to the better known Huxleys bank. Note how the tackle is laid out close to hand.

The River Avon at Evesham and Hampton Ferry still plays host to some of the biggest matches in the angling calendar, both open matches and top-class, invitation-only events which, as always, gain a lot of media interest and recognition. Because of this, the venue receives a great deal of attention – not just on match days but also during the week when anglers visit to practise methods and sharpen up their technique. Naturally, these tend to be very high-class anglers and the fish in the Avon in this area are well educated and far from easy to catch. The casual observer could be forgiven for assuming that the venue was not a prolific one, but that is not the case.

The river teems with fish. Catching them is the hard part, and this, plus the high-class field that any match at Evesham attracts makes the matches there very difficult to win.

Regulars to the venue are always searching for that extra edge that will see them into the frame, and on any day of the week there are liable to be several anglers busy experimenting with different approaches. The day that I arranged to meet Sammy on the venue unfortunately coincided with some absolutely vile weather, so it was not until midday that we actually started to fish. Sammy picked out a couple of pegs that he knew, on the opposite bank to

Huxley's café, a short walk from his caravan and away from some of the practising
match anglers who would inevitably want
to know what he was doing and if he was
catching.

Before we started, Sammy explained
that the chub had not, as yet, started to
show in any numbers, at least not to waggler tactics, and pole methods seemed to be
working best of all. Roach, skimmers and
the odd chub or two would be our main
target, with gudgeon likely to keep us busy
in between proper fish. The main line of
attack on the pole would be at about eight
metres, fishing line to hand – quite a feasible
method in view of the depth that might be
expected at that distance. The pegs that
Sammy selected for our practice were permanent numbers 137 and 139, both fair
pegs with the latter generally the better of
the two.

In common with a lot of English venues
in the late 1980s, the pole is very much an
in method on the River Avon, with the
Evesham/Hampton Ferry length a real
stronghold. It did cross my mind that
the pole might be being pressed into use
simply because it was there, as there had
been reports of anglers using it in situations
where it was not really the best option.
The current term for this is 'pole-itis', but
Sammy was quick to deny that he was a
sufferer from this disorder.

He feels that the pole gives better bait
presentation on a great many of the pegs
and a smaller percentage of missed bites.
He thinks that the reason for the latter is
twofold. Firstly, the pole puts the angler in
more direct contact, which means that
reaction to a bite is almost instantaneous,
so there should be very little slack line to be
picked up, as can happen with the conventional stick float and secondly, a relatively
smaller movement of the pole is required
to set the hock.

The type of pole floats being used also

tend to produce more hittable bites, with
the slender bristle proving much more sensitive and giving the angler plenty of pre-
warning. However, Sammy did point out
that he still saw quite a few anglers who
insisted of having some portion of the
body of the float visible as well as the
bristle, in which case they might just as
well use a conventional stickfloat with all
of its disadvantages.

Sammy's choice of pole also interested
me, especially as he told me that it was his
third in as many seasons in an attempt to
get one that was just right. He had eventually settled for a Maver Litium pole
which, at eleven metres, was one of the
lightest that I had handled. It was also very
rigid, and had the type of put-over joints
which I prefer. It was not a cheap item, but
looked to be a case of getting what you pay
for. I could see how Sammy was easily able
to fish all day with such a pole, although he
did say that it had its limitations.

The pole was ideal for light fishing
where odd bonus fish might be expected.
The Avon and most canals would suit it
down to the ground. However, he did feel
that it might suffer if exposed to the hand-
to-line fishing carried out in Ireland, or
some of the heavier Trent-style fishing. I
cringed inwardly when I thought of using
such a pole on a venue like Theale pits! My
pole, a trusty Tri Cast Maestro, had been
one of Sammy's earlier choices. However,
he had eventually decided that its weight
reduced his effectiveness over long periods,
especially when used at full stretch.
Accordingly, he had looked around for a
lighter pole but with the similar stiff action.

A Shimano had come and gone fairly
rapidly before he settled on the Litium, a
choice which he did not regret. To increase
his versatility with the pole, Sammy had
started to construct another Maver Litium,
this time by purchasing it a couple of
sections at a time. When I saw him, he had

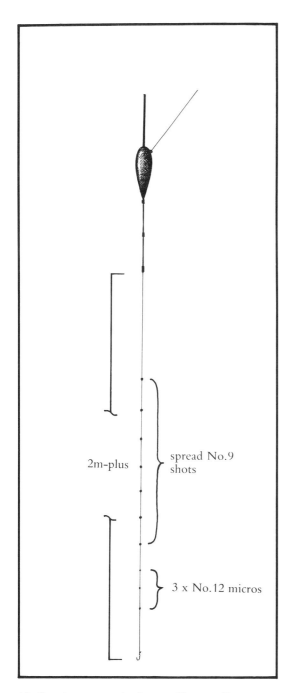

My first rig set-up on the Avon at Hampton Ferry.

2m-plus

spread No.9 shots

3 x No.12 micros

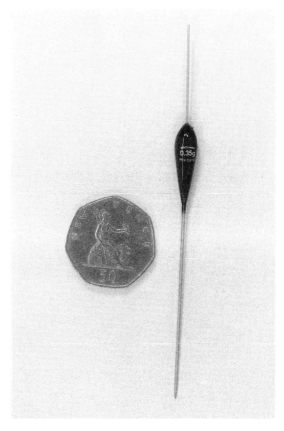

I used this pattern of float for my first session on the Warwickshire Avon. It was far too light for that job at only 0.50g.

one complete pole plus the top eight metres of another, so he was well on the way to achieving his aim. This, of course, afforded him the luxury of two rigs with slightly different shotting patterns, or identical ones with different breaking strain hook-links – the ideal solution for those moments in a match when an angler thinks 'I wonder what would happen if?'

Sometimes the changes just mentioned can take a bit of nerve to effect, especially if the angler is continuing to pick up an odd fish or two. A change might lead to him catching less quickly or not at all, or reduce the size of fish that he is catching. The dual set-up allows some flexibility in these circumstances.

I decided that the best way for me to learn anything constructive would be to let Sammy have the better of the two pegs so that I could watch someone doing things correctly. Sammy told me that my swim would be just over two metres deep on the line that I would be fishing. Plumbing the depth, I found that he was spot on. His peg was slightly deeper, although there was not much to choose between them as far as this was concerned. Floatwise, Sammy advised something between 0.50g and 1.0g, the shotting of which was optional. What he meant was that he quite often shotted his rigs up with strings of size 8 shot in the stick-float style, bunching them together if he felt the need for a bulk to get the bait down quickly. Alternatively, he sometimes used shaped tungsten tubing as a kind of olivette, with only the bare minimum of conventional shot as droppers.

Sammy's pole floats for the Avon were home-made and considerably larger than shop-bought counterparts that would take the same amount of weight. His floats, though, had heavy alloy stems, making them very stable. By contrast, I decided to use a 0.50g Clegg float, balsa body on a cane stem, with number 9 shots strung out stick float fashion. My reason for choosing this set-up rather than duplicating Sammy's 0.75g rig with tungsten tube bulk was to see how the two methods differed. Also, the river looked to be very sluggish and I quite fancied the idea of catching a fish or two on the drop.

Another surprise was in store for me when Sammy told me what bait he was going to use. I had always associated the river Avon, and Evesham in particular, with maggots, both as feed and hookbait. However, Sammy was going to feed casters and fish a red maggot on the hook to

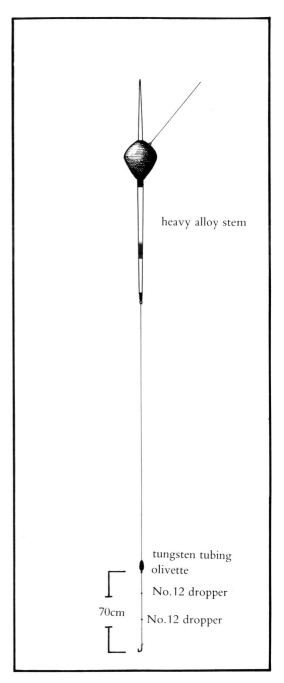

heavy alloy stem

tungsten tubing olivette

No.12 dropper

70cm

No.12 dropper

Sammy Mann's home-made 0.75g pole float shotted with tungsten tubing.

This float would have been an improvement, although still rather light for the depth of water in my swim.

start, switching to the caster now and again in the hope of a better fish or two. Again, I differed and opted to feed maggots and hemp, fishing maggot on the size 22 hook to 0.34kg nylon – normal tackle for the Avon according to Sammy.

Before we started, Sammy warned me not to overfeed my swim – a maximum of a litre of maggots would be all that I would need. Naturally then, I started off quite lightly on the loose feed – half a dozen maggots every cast as soon as the pole float hit the water. I soon found out that I had been wrong about the sluggish flow. Although far from being a fast-flowing

river in that area, the Avon still has some movement. What had fooled me were the floating leaves remaining almost stationary on the surface. A slight upstream wind was causing this and, below the surface, the river was moving appreciably quicker.

However, I was still able to attract bites, although these seemed to be coming from gudgeon or minnows in the main, not the dace and roach that I had been led to expect. Obviously some of my loose feed was reaching these fish, but I did notice that some of the maggots were being snapped up just under the surface. I suspected bleak, and was proved right when I caught one. I stepped up the feed to a dozen maggots every cast to compensate for the ones being picked off by the bleak on the way down. After three-quarters of an hour or so I caught my first dace – only a small one but hopefully a hint of better things to come. The roach were still proving elusive.

Not so for Sammy who had netted a fish of near on half a kilo, plus a couple of smaller ones. He had also had a brace of reasonable chub and some dace. Checking my terminal tackle over, he advised me to bulk my shots up in the style of an olivette and fish with just two or three droppers below. This I did, but still the roach proved reluctant and an hour later I still hadn't caught one. Sammy's run of fish had slowed a little, and I scrounged a few casters off him to see if any better fish would respond in my peg. Again, I fed them quite lightly (a dozen or so at maximum), keeping to the same size 22 hook to fine nylon. On only my third cast, the float went away almost on the drop. I lifted into the fish, and instead of another gudgeon spiralling its way up through the water, the number 3 Zim elastic stretched its way out of the pole tip. The fish bumped around for a few seconds before allowing itself to be drawn towards the landing net – a superb roach, just shy of half a kilo.

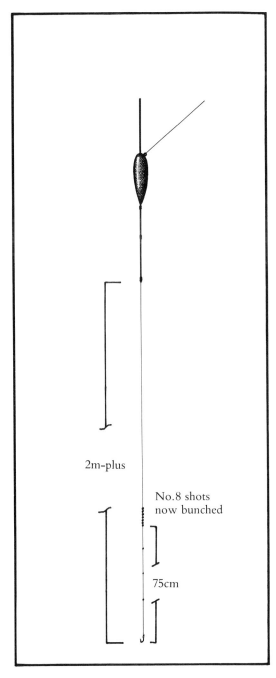

2m-plus

No.8 shots
now bunched

75cm

Sammy Mann's adjustment to my rig at Hampton Ferry.

A couple of casts later, I hooked an even bigger roach, only to lose it when the hook pulled. Naturally this slowed sport down with them, but meantime I landed a big dace and a chub of similar size to the first roach. Obviously, casters attracted the better fish. Just as the fishing was becoming very interesting, the heavens opened and Sammy and I decided to call it a day. In what had been a fairly brief session, Sammy had landed somewhere between three and four kilos, easily doubling my weight. However, we had both learned a great deal and Sammy, in particular, was looking forward to the mid-week match on the opposite bank next day.

Because of our results, especially the way my swim had burst into life, Sammy decided to base his attack on the caster as the river was still not quite fishing up to its full potential and the odd bonus fish that the caster might bring could well be the difference between winning and coming nowhere. Sammy still stuck to this line of attack even when he drew what was possibly quite a safe peg to fish the maggot on – peg 89. It has a history of producing good catches, and the temptation to play the percentages must have been great. However, Sammy reasoned that he had little to lose by starting on the caster, especially as recent results with it had been so good.

Unfortunately he was not so lucky with the pole option. Peg 89 is rather overgrown and a stick float is the only alternative for the close-in line. The depth of around a couple of metres on the stick float line is ideal by Evesham standards, especially during the autumn, so Sammy was confident of catching a few fish. He decided to feed two lines for his stick float – one only a metre and a half from the near bank, the other some eight metres or so out.

Again, the float was a home-made special – a wire stemmed stick float with a shotting

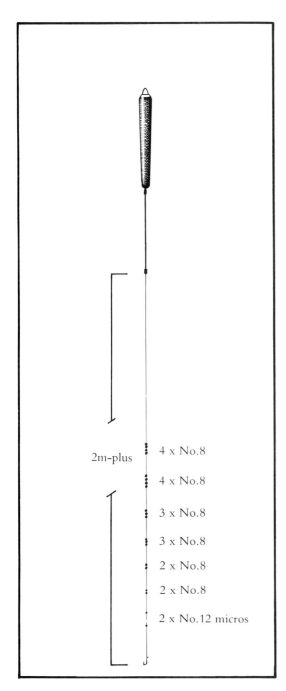

2m-plus

4 x No.8

4 x No.8

3 x No.8

3 x No.8

2 x No.8

2 x No.8

2 x No.12 micros

Sammy Mann's stick float rig for the River Avon at Hampton Ferry.

capacity of around seven number 4s, although this was broken down very small indeed. Sammy has always used very long hooklinks, somewhere in the region of seventy-five centimetres, which, by coincidence, is something that I do too, unless I am fishing a very fine hooklink of less than 0.35kg where I use a much shorter one. The reason for this is that I do not like to weaken fine line any further by pinching shots on to it. However, Sammy was using a 0.50kg hooklink to size 20 hook to start, and he placed three size 10 shots on the hooklink.

The rest of his shotting was broken down, in size 8 shots, paired, then trebled, then quadrupled, all on the bottom two thirds of his terminal tackle. This was because he did not expect too many bites on the drop at this time of year and thought that the improved bait presentation with the lead well down would catch him more, and better fish. As he expected, gudgeon were the first species to show, but by catching a few fish from each of his chosen lines of attack, he was able to keep bites coming quite steadily. Soon a pattern began to emerge, the longer each line was left without being fished, the more instant results became when he switched his attention to it. A couple of reasonable skimmers boosted his weight quite handily and the gudgeon averaging out at around forty to the kilo were a very nice stamp to be picking up on a regular basis.

The fish still weren't coming quite fast enough though, and a drop down to a finer 0.45kg hooklink was called for. This brought an improvement and the odd roach started to be tempted into having a go. These weren't quite as big as the previous day's, but at 250–330g apiece they were a handy bonus. By the midpoint of the match, Sammy had worked his way to a substantial lead, but still he felt that he was not catching quickly enough, although he had started to pick a few small chub.

He considered going even finer on the hooklink and switching to a size 22 hook in search of a few extra fish. However, he decided against this in favour of catching what fish he could on the slightly heavier tackle, saving the fine gear for a late rally if need be. This proved to be a fortuitous gamble as almost immediately he struck into a good sized chub that tipped the scales at more than a kilo. It would have proved quite a handful on even finer tackle. Another couple of decent chub set the seal on the match and Sammy ran out a convincing winner with 7kg 527g. His quartet of big chub accounted for nearly half of his total, scaling 3kg 452g between them, the biggest going 1kg 360g.

The runner-up was well adrift with 4kg 471g which amply illustrated Sammy's dominance of the match. Apart from shallowing up by a few centimetres at one stage, Sammy had made very few tackle adjustments. His swim had a fairly even depth so major changes between his two lines of attack were not needed and switching lines gave him all the variety that he needed to keep the fish interested. The pre-match practice had certainly paid dividends for Sammy, although he was quick to point out that the peg had been an exceptionally good one to draw on the day. Having said that, his margin of victory proved to me that perhaps his ability might have had something to do with the outcome too!

Even though Sammy had won that Wednesday Open he still had a couple of day's holiday left that he could devote to practice. The caravan had turned up trumps again, allowing him maximum time on the venue. Significantly, a cold snap on Wednesday night put a real dampener on sport the following day and Sammy struggled for a couple of kilos. However, he was

fishing what he knew to be difficult pegs, simply to find out what the possibilities were from them, and whether there might be a method that would put him in with a chance, even on these swims.

Friday saw another cold evening slowing sport down, although this time the fish were marginally more willing to feed, having had time to adjust to the lower temperature. It was interesting that anglers arriving in time for a start just after midday were enjoying the best sport. Obviously the slight rise in temperature around the middle of the day was bringing fish on to the food. Also noticeable was an increase in the number of chub willing to feed, and Sammy felt that a fair weight might be needed if these conditions were duplicated during the match.

Because of this he again favoured the White House area, which had been the scene of his Wednesday success, although the pegs opposite to our Tuesday practice pegs also had a lot of potential for both chub and roach. Indeed, this had proved to be one of the best areas on the Friday afternoon with a couple of ten kilo-plus nets being a feature. Of one thing Sammy was absolutely certain – with the calibre of angler that had turned up for this match we needed to draw well to be in with any sort of a chance and, of course, I needed to draw an appreciably better peg than Sammy to be in with an equal chance.

One good point about the match was that it was scheduled to be fished during the warmest part of the day, with a starting time of 11 a.m. With this in mind, Sammy thought that the waggler had every chance of being the winning method, especially as it had proved so effective the previous day. There was a tangible air of nervous anticipation at the draw. I let Sammy go first before I decided to see what fate had in store for me.

Sammy drew peg 38, a short walk from

My peg on the Huxleys Open at Hampton Ferry on the Warwickshire Avon – number 43. Not much of a history of big weights from this one.

the car-park and one of the deepest areas on the river – not quite what he had in mind as a potential winner. However, he had drawn the peg once before, several years previously, and had landed six chub for a weight of around six kilos – an excellent average size. That, he said, was one aspect that hadn't changed, and if he caught a chub from this peg, he expected it to be a large one. More recently, he had drawn the peg next door and had latched on to one of a kilo and a half in the last half hour of the match, to win the section. So, at least he had something to fish for.

I was not very far away (space is at a premium at Hampton Ferry), on peg 43, again a very deep peg with few redeeming features. Its only saving grace was that Sammy would be near at hand to answer any questions that I might have, and at least I would be able to fish in a similar fashion as our pegs were almost identical. Sammy still favoured the pole in our area, although he also felt that a few casts on the waggler would be a good idea at the start, just on the off chance of picking up a quick but simple chub. In view of the depth, Sammy advised me to fish well off bottom, something that it would be easy to do as I was faced with over four metres of water in mid-river, and my feed would be lucky to hit bottom within the confines of my swim, even on the sluggish waters of the Avon.

My swim was a similar depth on the eight-metre pole line. Far too deep, according to Sammy but, at worst, he felt that we might catch a roach or two. As is often the case with such pegs, Sammy told me that they tended to be quite fair with a drop of extra water on, but in spite of the river carrying what looked to be an ideal colour, the level did not look to be in our favour. Because my peg was only a short walk from the car-park, I had plenty of time to tackle up, plumb the depth and generally survey the river. I did have a small bed of reeds in the downstream part of my swim and toyed with the idea of fishing tight up against it. Sammy had told me that John Sherwood, a regular winner on the venue, often did well by fishing the stick float down that line. It sounded a simple ploy but, as Sammy pointed out, John was the only angler who appeared to be able to make that technique work. Accordingly, I flirted with the idea of setting up a stick float rod but abandoned it as complicating matters too much.

Around me, I could hear the mutterings and grumblings of anglers who would much rather have been elsewhere on the river. Being a relative stranger, I was not at the disadvantage of knowing the venue too well, a factor that can sometimes leave you beaten before you start. A great deal of grief seemed to be being expended over Shakespeare's Dave Harrell drawing peg 86, apparently a very hot peg, now with an equally hot angler on it. Sammy was of the opinion that Dave would fish the waggler and win the match from that draw, and said that the combination of a World Championship standard angler and a good peg is hard to beat anywhere.

The main thoughts that were going through my mind were concerned with catching an early chub to give me a flying start. So my first task was setting up a suitable rig for this. I decided on a 3AAA double insert waggler, locked with the AAA shots and with only two number 10 shots down the line. Initially, I set the float at about two metres – well under depth but

as good a starting-point as any. At the sharp end, I used a size 20 to 0.45kg nylon – perhaps a little heavier than is currently popular, but there is always the chance of one daft fish early on, and I was determined to land it if it came my way.

On the pole line, I found that Sammy had again been exactly right, and was glad to have chosen a 0.75g Clegg special to cope with the depth. This time I opted for a bulk and dropper pattern, as the shirt button shotting had proved to be a waste of time in practice. Again I decided to start with a 20 to 0.45kg on the same premise as the waggler method, any early bonus fish might prove vital. Bait-wise I was well prepared – a litre and a half of casters, and the same of maggots (white), and hemp. I also had a couple of kilos of cereal groundbait, some of the Van Den Eynde range and a few red maggots as change hookbaits.

The pole is now a favourite method at Hampton Ferry, and the two anglers each side of me started the match on it. Both appeared to be feeding maggots on the pole line, and both picked up a few minnows and gudgeon almost straight away. I decided to take Sammy's advice and give the waggler twenty minutes or so, although I also fed in a few casters on the pole line in readiness. The waggler brought an instant response as I loose fed maggots by catapult half-way across the river. However, the bites were impossible to hit and I suspected that the culprits might be small fish. Altering the depth seemed to make matters no better, and I was still unable to hit bites when I got them. On every occasion the maggot returned unmarked.

Eventually I made contact with one of the mystery fish and, as I suspected, it turned out to be a bleak weighing only a few grams. Further changes of depth and shotting failed to attract a bite from a proper fish, so I decided that the time

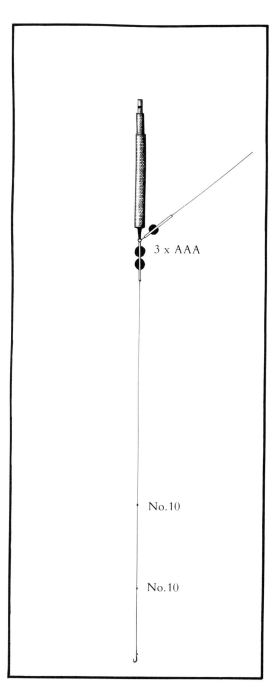

The double insert waggler that I tackled up with at Hampton Ferry. Ideal for catching fish on the drop on a venue of sluggish flow, 3 AAA capacity gives good distance potential.

Double insert peacock waggler. My rig for the Avon at Hampton Ferry.

was right to switch to the pole. Perhaps naively, I expected an instant response, and was rather taken aback when I didn't get it. The match was just over half an hour old and I had been dripping a few casters into the swim from the outset. A switch to red maggot on the hook did attract a bite but even with the best will in the world, I couldn't see myself getting into the frame by catching minnows.

The anglers to each side of me were also struggling, and they too seemed able only to catch minnows. Now it was their turn to switch methods, and both swapped to mini swimfeeders. This was a method that Sammy had discounted as a major ploy, and certainly the two anglers did not seem to be enjoying much action. Meanwhile, I adjusted the depth on my pole rig and steadily dripped a few casters into the swim on each cast. After about an hour I still had only a bleak and a minnow to show for my efforts. Nevertheless, I still felt that the caster swim might come to life.

Repeated switches to maggot only attracted bites from minnows. Not even gudgeon could be tempted by my pole rig. I decided that a short walk down the bank to see how Sammy was faring might be in order. Just as I was contemplating this, and within a few minutes of each other, the anglers each side of me struck into fish on the swimfeeder. At around three hundred grams, these were not really big fish but, compared to what I had in my net, they were gigantic. I scrubbed my visit to Sammy and hurriedly set up a mini feeder myself.

This too had the size 20 to 0.45kg at the business end, and I was confident of attracting a bite or two. It wasn't too long before my partners had another net fish apiece, and I was still waiting for my first bite. This didn't worry me too much as they had been fishing the method for a longer period and had obviously estab-lished a catching area by dropping the

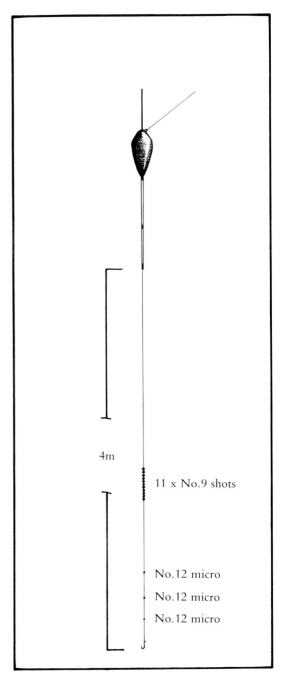

Dick Clegg's pole float, bulk shotted, for the match.

feeder into the same spot. I had yet to build up my area. As I expected, this took the best part of an hour – approximately as long as it had taken my next door neighbours. Unfortunately, when I did get a bite it was only from a gudgeon, hardly anything to get excited about.

Meantime, the angler on my left had been unlucky to lose a big chub that had snagged him on the way in. At this stage I decided to see what Sammy had to offer in the way of advice. He too was struggling, although he had caught a few silver fish on the pole, a couple of small roach and a reasonable skimmer had hinted at better things to come but had flattered to deceive. The swimfeeder was holding a certain attraction in his mind too.

I had only been back at my peg for a few minutes when my concentration was again disturbed by the angler on my left. This time he seemed to be getting the better of a struggle with another big chub, which miraculously transformed itself into half a kilo of angry eel as he prepared to land it. This duly completed, he looked to be a good bet for the section. I was still biteless on the swimfeeder so I decided to risk another half hour on the waggler which, as it turned out, only made matters worse. This time I couldn't even attract bites from bleak and the chance of a chub looked remote. Changing the depth every other cast made no difference whatsoever and I decided that the waggler had had its last fling.

Another attempt to make things happen on the pole met with complete indifference, even fining down to 0.35kg breaking strain hooklinks and a size 22 hook failed to bring any upturn in sport. The swimfeeder began to look like the only option. I sat it out on the swimfeeder for the remainder of the match. Bites did become a little more regular, but only from gudgeon. Worse still, at one stage I actually caught a

stickleback on this rig. What was that doing at the bottom of five metres of water in the middle of the River Avon? More to the point, why wasn't a big chub or perch trying to make a meal of it?

Finally, I adopted desperation tactics with the swimfeeder and the size 24 hook to 0.30kg nylon. Again, gudgeon and the occasional minnow were the only takers. The only saving grace was that this switch to very light gear didn't attract a cardiac arresting bite from a big kilo-and-a-half chub that would have had to be played very gingerly. By the end of the match, the two anglers either side of me had weights of one-and-a-half to two kilos, and had added a couple more net fish apiece towards the end of the match. My paltry few fish wouldn't even have broken the half kilo mark. I was so disgusted that I didn't bother to weigh them.

Sammy was similarly stricken, and at the end, the only difference in our catches was the small skimmer and brace of roach that he had caught on the pole. Obviously, I was keen to find out what we had done wrong, although I suspected our biggest mistake had been made at the draw bag. I also felt that our early foray on the waggler had prevented us both from catching on the swimfeeder. Although we didn't feed the waggler line heavily, we were introducing as much in one helping as two or three casts with the mini feeder. Worse, we were obviously spreading that feed around more, and even in that depth of water I am sure that some of the feed was reaching bottom within the confines of our swims. This meant that those fish which may have been willing to move to investigate the feed coming from a feeder, instead had the feed delivered to them. Their hunger sated, they didn't have to accept our swimfeedered offerings.

When I quizzed Sammy about our perhaps starting on the wrong method he did concede that it was a gamble which might have backfired. However, he said that he would be willing to bet on the waggler being the winning method. This proved to be exactly right, with Shakespeare's Dave Harrell repeating Sammy's mid-week feat by slaughtering a high-class field. His 8kg 744g catch was comfortably ahead of the chasing pack with the runner-up netting just over five kilos. The bulk of Dave's catch was taken on the waggler, with his best brace of fish going a handy three kilos between them. The same area that had provided Sammy with his mid-week success had come up trumps again, this time peg 86 for the winner and peg 85 for the runner-up.

As far as the waggler was concerned, we had the right method but the wrong pegs to make it work. The important difference, though, was that Dave had worked in reverse to our plan – starting off close in before switching to the waggler to sew the match up. However, he had obviously put some feed in on the waggler line before making the change so the reverse style may not have been quite so good on our pegs after all.

What I had learned on these most recent visits to the Avon at Hampton Ferry was that, in some respects, the river had not changed much in the years since I had last visited it. Certainly, the catches seemed to be higher then, but the fish on that section have never been too easy to catch. Obviously, each new trend revives catches for a while, and there have been plenty of new trends on that length. However, none of them keep the fish on the boil forever and there, more than anywhere else, the match angler has to keep one jump ahead. Like the River Trent at Burton Joyce and the Witham at Kirkstead, the fish have a sixth sense which tells them when it is a match day. They all offer some of the hardest fishing in the match angling world.

My last visits to the Avon had been around ten years previously, and I had done quite well in the matches that I had fished, at one stage picking up minor prizes in three consecutive visits. However, I had drawn very well on those occasions, and really should perhaps have done better. One match in particular springs to mind where I switched to the waggler too late in the match, catching three chub in my last three casts to get amongst the money. The chub tended to be smaller then, certainly not the kilo-plus fish which seem a feature nowadays.

That period also coincided with a great deal of interest in the swimfeeder, a method that was carrying all before it on the venue. On my very first visit to Evesham, I had to borrow a swimfeeder rod to be able to fish my peg. In spite of my endeavours, rather than because of them, I managed to scrape a section win. I also seem to remember beating Sammy off the next peg in those early days, but as I said earlier, I was drawing very very well, and one peg either way can make a big difference at Evesham.

Looking back, perhaps the most satisfying performance that I put in on the venue came one freezing winter's day on a swim that I didn't fancy at all. The rod rings were icing up which meant that casting was difficult, and fishing the stick float, almost impossible. Coupled with this, an overhanging tree on my upstream side meant that I couldn't feed my swim quite as I liked, and on the tight pegging there, I was feeding the downstream angler's swim instead of my own. Not surprisingly, it didn't take him long to start catching but, as with all of the anglers, he was struggling to cast his waggler any distance as his rod rings iced up.

Eventually, after an hour's hard effort, I decided on a tackle change that was to get me fishing with some conviction. I switched floats for a bodied 4½SSSG waggler which had a slender peacock quill insert. I still kept the shotting down the line fairly light at two sixes and two eights, but it was rather heavier than normal, and intended to slow the float down still further. The reason that I changed to a heavier float was that the greater weight made it easier to cast. Logical really, but, with the rod rings still icing up, I had very little problem propelling the heavy float to where I wanted it, whereas the usual 3AAA float was reluctant to pull the line through the rod rings.

I also found that by firing my bait out almost at water-level I was able to get some feed into my swim, and it was not too long before I caught a small roach. A couple more followed, which meant that I had caught up with the angler downstream of me, and with two hours now gone I was in a much better frame of mind. Then the major stroke of luck, which made all the difference, occurred. I struck at a bite no different to any other and was rewarded with the rod arching over in an alarming fashion. I played, or was played by, what felt like a decent fish for quite some minutes, although the way in which it fought seemed rather strange. As it eventually neared the net, I saw that I had been correct in my instinctive guess that the fish had been foul-hooked, right in the root of the tail. Nevertheless, a half-kilo chub was a handsome bonus on that freezing day. The next hours saw a slight increase in temperature, and I managed to add a few more roach to my total before a drop in temperature during the last hour saw bites cease altogether.

I finished the match with 1kg 480g for sixth, which wasn't a bad result considering the conditions. Strangely enough, that match was won from peg 39, so Sammy had indeed been correct when he had suggested that the area had some form. But,

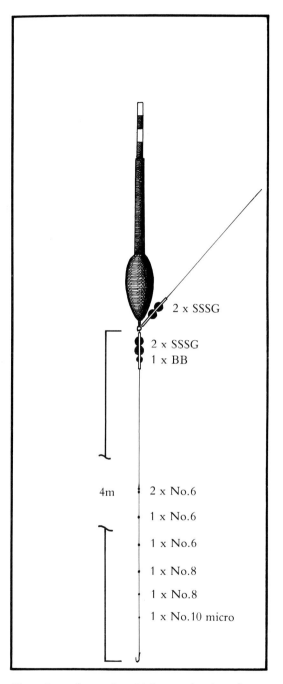

Heavy inserted peacock and balsa waggler rig used at Evesham because of icing difficulty.

This big inserted waggler has won me a few bob over the years. I pressed it into service on the Warwickshire Avon when conditions demanded it.

the angler who did the business that day was Paul Downes which proved to be another case of an exceptionally good angler turning up trumps on the Avon.

One thing about the venue that I did find a little disconcerting was the pleasure anglers' view of the river on my most recent visit. Obviously, it must have been a convenient venue for them to get to (although most of the Avon looks as if it is solid with fish, which attracts anglers from far and wide), but, their catches didn't seem to bear any resemblance to their enthusiasm.

They seemed to be very glad with a catch of a couple of kilos, and anything around four or five kilos sent them into near ecstasy. On my local river, such catches wouldn't merit a second look, but then again, I suppose that half of the fun is catching the fish from the Avon. They require so much guile that even with only a few bites to show, you at least feel that you have had a day's fishing.

5 John McCarthy

John McCarthy is one of angling's most colourful characters, never far away from the centre of any action. Any angler lacking in the slightest in self-confidence must find drawing next to him a nightmare. Usually, his confidence allows him to describe just how he is going to win the match, and what records he might decide to break along the way! However, this effusive nature of his has been known to work against him, as it can goad the adjacent anglers into ever-greater efforts to beat him. It can also draw fish-scaring crowds of people which also serves to make his task harder.

John is one of those tackle dealers who manage to do quite nicely, and his hard work since he entered the trade mirrors his match angling outlook. Now getting on a bit at 42 years of age, John is still as keen as ever. However, the enthusiasm of youth has, inevitably, been tempered by a yen for the good things in life which, in John's match angling parlance, means plenty of fish. You will not find John blue and shivering on a wintry river bank awaiting a bite from a dry net-saving gudgeon.

Winter league team fishing is now a thing of the past, but in earlier years John was an important member of several successful outfits, notably Dorking, the Team and Del Cac. International honours beckoned when John was included in Home International matches in Ireland, doing himself proud on venues that were almost tailor-made for his attacking style. Therefore, I wasn't too surprised at John's choice of venue, or the species which offered the greatest chance of success.

Carp seldom figure as a main target species in Midland and Northern matches, and are usually seen as a fortuitous capture, not least because they can be difficult to land! However, they are an increasingly popular quarry in Southern match circles, with pleasure anglers equally keen to try their luck on some of the prolific carp lakes. The winning weights on these venues naturally tend towards the high side – right up John's street, although he was quick to point out the fishing was not a case of quantity over quality, and anglers had to be adept at landing carp once they had hooked them.

Another thing that I learned, at an early stage, was the propensity of Southern anglers to methodise venues. Some carp lakes respond to heavy groundbait, others to loose feed only; some to float, others feeder. What rapidly became clear was that Dorking's runaway win in the 1988 Angling Times Winter League final at Mallory Park Lakes was no fluke. The Southern contingent have a head's start over their Northern rivals and I was keen to pick up what I could from their specialised techniques.

As I mentioned earlier, John's all-action attacking style seemed as good a starting-point as any, and his experience on a wide variety of carp venues made him the ideal choice for a quick tutorial on the species. I was also keen to learn the secrets that had kept him ahead of the pack, making him a consistent winner rather than an occasional one – some aspects of the carp approach might have applications in other spheres.

Such is the boom in popularity of carp that John predicted a rapid growth in the number of venues holding enough numbers to make them an interesting angling proposition. Typically, he was already on the look-out for a suitable pool to buy and run as a going concern, catering for both match and pleasure anglers. I am sure that John is right in the latter case as there must still be a high percentage of pleasure anglers who have never seen, let alone caught, a carp. Carp obviously have some peculiarities as a match species, not the least being their unquenchable desire to remain in their natural environment and their aptitude for putting the maximum distance between themselves and the angler in the minimum time.

John's chosen venue was Theale pits, an old ballast working near to Reading, and an established favourite with London-based anglers. The venue is strictly controlled by Cove Angling Club and many anglers' only chance to fish it is by way of an open match. Accordingly, demand for tickets is high and some top-class anglers are attracted. Matches on the venue are by no means easy to win. Competitors must have a good range of techniques at their disposal and show a high level of competence in them all.

Carp have not always been the dominant species at Theale. Indeed, they only became a serious factor in match results around 1986. However, Theale has always been a big-weight venue as, prior to the carp explosion, matches were won with fifteen to twenty kilos of small tench or 'bars of soap', as the Theale regulars call them. Matches are split between the so-called large and small lakes, with separate competitions on each. This practice started as it became obvious that the large lake was

dominating the results and that anglers unlucky enough to draw the small lake had little chance. I can think of plenty of venues where a similar system might give encouragement to the less fortunate.

A winner-take-all pool does provide additional attraction for the overall winner, and by one of those quirks of fate common to all sports, the first occasion when the match was split saw an angler on the small pool scoop the top prize!

Although carp took over quite suddenly at Theale, there is a wide size band for anglers to tackle. Typically, though, most of the heavier catches contain a high proportion of fish around the one kilo mark, although fish of six or seven kilos are not unknown. Averaging less than one metre in depth for the most part, and harbouring plenty of snags in most swims, Theale does not give up its carp without a fierce struggle and tackle is tested to its limits. Being the type of creatures that they are, carp love features, by which I mean reed beds, underwater obstructions and overhanging branches. Theale has an abundance of them.

The cold, wet summer of 1988 certainly didn't bode well for carp fishing, and the anglers taking part in the first of the matches that I visited were not over-enthused about the chances of big catches. Nevertheless, John had arrived at the match geared up with plenty of bait, just in case. Around seven litres of large white maggots plus three litres of pinkies made up his bait requirement. Obviously, the fish were going to be well fed. His reasoning was simple – if the fish weren't in his peg at the start of the match, he would try to make sure that they were by the end of it with constant feeding. He did point out, however, that this was more of a tactic for the open water swims, and less bait might be needed for a more featured swim which would tend to hold carp anyway.

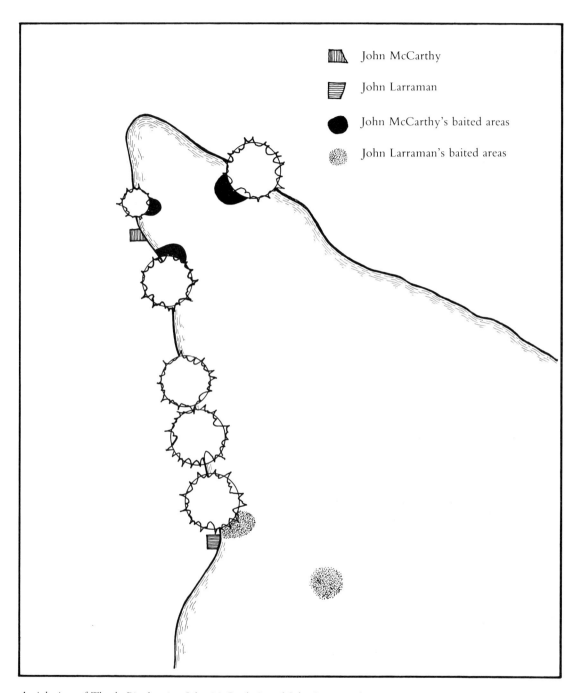

John McCarthy

John Larraman

John McCarthy's baited areas

John Larraman's baited areas

Aerial view of Theale Pit showing John McCarthy's and John Larraman's pegs.

John really fancied peg 28 on the large lake, but was unlucky to see it plucked from the bag before his turn came. Number 52 saw him on the big lake though – a preferable position for his style of fishing, but not ideal as it turned out. Peg 52 was certainly rich in features, with overhanging bushes right, left and opposite of the corner in which it was situated.

Personally, I am not over keen on corner pegs in stillwaters, and John shared some of my reservations. I am always of the opinion that you can only catch what fish are there already, and the chances of drawing any more into the swim are not good. However, if there are plenty of fish there, you normally only have to share them with one other angler. In John's case, this was not a problem as the angler opposite him on the corner was shielded by the overhanging bushes that I mentioned earlier. Another plus factor was the facing wind. This was going to make life uncomfortable, but there was a very good chance that it would encourage fish to that corner of the lake. All in all, it was a pretty fair draw, especially as the area had a history of good catches, with peg 53 particularly noted.

Prior to the start of the match, John mentioned a few anglers whom he thought might pose a threat. John Larraman and Tommy Hiller were amongst the favourites and by coincidence, John 'Lasher' Larraman was pegged nearby on peg 54. This is a more open peg, comfortably situated and offering multiple options by virtue of having near side cover too. Back on peg 52, John had decided to base his opening attack around the less menacing looking of his near side bushes, which was situated to his left and further towards the corner. To give himself more options, he set up a couple of tackles – one a straight ledger rod with just enough weight to flick across the opposite side, the other a float rod sporting a 2BB waggler, the running line giving more variety than a simple pole set-up which might have been thought more appropriate so close in.

The match did not start particularly well for John. Feeding heavily, he soon attracted fish into his swim, but was equally quickly plagued by line bites as the fish milled around after the loose feed. This, I was told, was quite normal but, if the fish failed to settle into a steady feeding routine, could cause a problem. Worse was to come when the first real bite that John had resulted in a lively fish finding a snag and snapping the hooklink. At least it showed that the top men have their trials and tribulations as well as the rest of us. The first hour saw only one small carp and two or three small tench and roach put into the keepnet but, as John was at pains to point out, one good hour could change all that.

Theale, it transpired, was a working anglers' venue, one which responded to anglers who kept busy with their feed and terminal tackle. Having said that, adjustments in shotting seemed few, and only changes of depth and, on some occasions, hook size were of importance. Because of the abundant snags, John had tackled up with 1.50kg reel line, 1kg hooklink and a forged 18-crystal hook completed the business end.

A visit to John Larraman, on peg 54, provided a contrast. Because his peg was more open, he had set up three tackles – a carbon pole teamed with number 8 Zim elastic, a waggler rod and a quivertip rod. The pole tackle consisted of a tiny fragment of peacock quill attached waggler-style, with no shots between float and hook. Line breaking strains were identical to John McCarthy's running line rig. This pole set-up was used for prospecting the area adjacent to a half-sunken bush immediately to John Larraman's left. However, he was also continuously feeding a more distant swim, some twenty

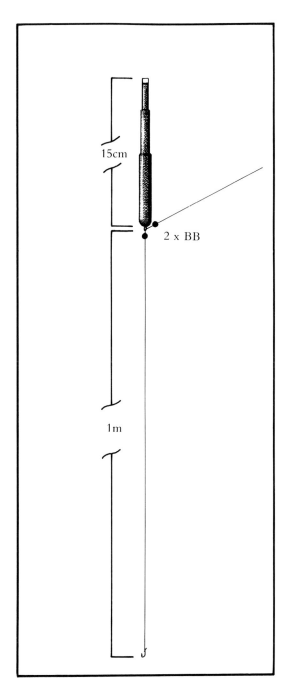

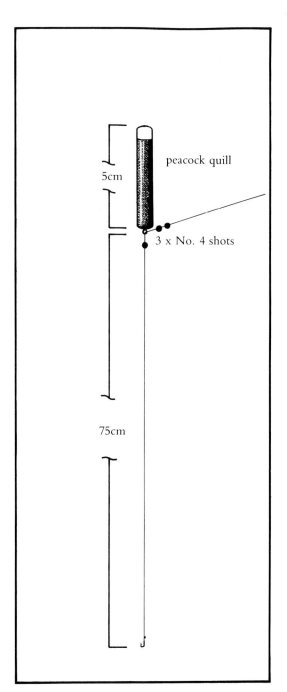

John McCarthy's double insert waggler rig for close-in fishing at Theale. Note that there is no shot 'down the line' below the float.

'Lasher' Larraman's pole rig at Theale.

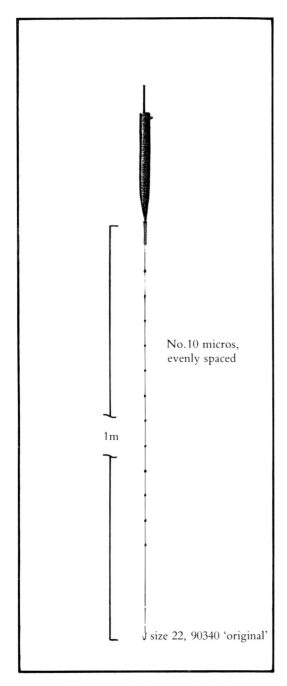

No.10 micros,
evenly spaced

1m

size 22, 90340 'original'

Kenny Collings' milo pole float rig on Theale's small lake.

metres out, by catapult, in readiness for a switch to waggler or swimfeeder.

It was obvious that he was catching at a much faster rate than John McCarthy, yet not quite fast enough to satisfy himself, with the result that he switched frequently from pole to rod in an attempt to keep up the catching rhythm and pick up a better stamp of fish. John McCarthy's prediction of a serious threat looked all too true, and I noted John Larraman down as a potential winner.

I also decided to pay the small pool a visit, after replaying the gloomy news to John, as I could by no means be certain of avoiding drawing there when I took my chance on the venue. Sport there seemed to be more consistent, with a higher proportion of anglers tangling with carp. With only a couple of hours left in the match, I settled behind Kenny Collings, drawn on peg 8, not very far from a sunken car. His tackle set-up was very interesting and incorporated a sensitive pole float fished close by a reed bed on rod and line. He had a pretty fair depth close in and had only a couple of kilos as I arrived.

However, almost as soon as I settled behind him, his swim burst into life and he began to hit into carp. Cleverly alternating between the reeds on his right and left he too began to show signs of winning. Interestingly, his terminal tackle was lighter than most with a tiny size 22 hook and 750g hooklink. Also, as light as his float was, he appeared to have the most lead down the line of any angler that I saw, having a string of number 10 micros evenly spaced between float and hook, the float being set at around one metre.

With just over an hour to go, I paid another fleeting visit to John Larraman, still catching well, and with that early advantage over the anglers who were only now starting to catch. Fortunately, John McCarthy was one of them, and in the last hour he made a spirited bid for the honours with a succession of carp including one around the two kilo mark. Sticking to his original plan throughout, he had indeed drawn some fish into his swim, but he felt that they had come just too late to do him any good. I was not so sure and felt that he wouldn't be too far away from a reward of some kind.

Unfortunately for John, his gloomy prediction was correct, his weight of 12.7kg being only enough for sixth place. As I half expected, John Larraman won the match with 14.3kg, more than a kilo clear of the runner-up. However, I was interested to see the chasing group all bunched around the twelve or thirteen kilo mark, six or seven anglers landing such catches, which hinted that mistakes could prove to be expensive. John was not pleased with himself after the match. One more fish would have seen him amongst the prizes, and three more would have won him the match. That early lost fish had come back to haunt him.

I had seen enough to realise that match fishing for carp was not as easy as the top men had made it seem, but perhaps the most telling piece of information came from John Larraman. Experience had taught him that carp rarely feed for the full five hours of a match in any one way or, more seriously, at any one depth. Presentation, therefore, is critical, along with an experimental nature if things aren't going exactly to plan. Putting this invaluable piece of information into perspective, it became obvious that I hadn't really seen John McCarthy at his best, as the peg that he had drawn had been rather too cramped to allow him full freedom of expression.

However, it had shown that his choice of exactly which area of his swim would offer him the best chance of catching competitively had been dead right. I am afraid that I may have been tempted to fish either the

Exactly the kind of float that Kenny Collings was using to such deadly effect on the running line at Theale. I certainly wouldn't have thought of it.

heavier features to the right of the peg, or the sunken bush opposite, in the hope of drawing a few fish from the more open area. I would probably have given little attention to the somewhat sparse cover on the left-hand side, which also seemed to offer no potential for drawing fish. During the plentiful quiet spells throughout the match, John had prospected the heavier cover to his right but had been unable to catch a fish there. The bush opposite looked to be too much of a gamble, and in his own words he wasn't struggling *that* much!

Nevertheless, he had continued to feed all of the three options right through to the end, wisely keeping his options open should the unthinkable happen and bites cease entirely on the main swim. His confidence had never wavered. He was certain, in his own mind, that come the end of the match he would not be very far away from the prizes. Both he and John Larraman reckoned that it was possible to win money from 90 per cent of the pegs on the venue, which must have had something to do with his confidence. There was a final factor which was a little difficult to quantify. This was the feel that he had for the venue, the factor which led him to concentrate his efforts in the part of the swim that he did.

The anglers that made mistakes on the venue were the ones who either gave up completely or who concentrated their energies in the wrong places, for too long. Even though Theale has the potential to produce big catches, the fish are usually of such a size that the angler does not need to be catching them constantly to put a good catch together. A good hour is all that is required.

Sticking to my task was something that I felt I could cope with, especially as I had seen just what could be achieved in a short space of time. In Kenny Collings' case, the carp had appeared, as if by magic, and boosted him up into the prize list. Choosing the right tactics was obviously going to be more difficult but, by taking my cue from John, I could at least keep two or three options open by constant feeding, hoping that at least one of them might respond. My main fear was that I might draw on a shoal of carp that started to go silly, that is come right up in the water and feed in an apparent frenzy. This, I was warned, could be the most frustrating thing of all – to be surrounded by feeding fish, yet unable to catch them.

Tacklewise, I felt that I could cope with the venue. I had in mind a pretty sturdy carbon match rod which I had purchased several years earlier, even before I had seen the venue. I was delighted to discover that John McCarthy used exactly the same model, one of the old Sundridge Kevin Ashurst rods. My tried and tested old glass rods would be sufficient for the swimfeeder fishing and well able to cope with the distances to be cast, as well as playing hard fighting fish. The local favourite pole for carp fishing was the Daiwa Pro Carbon, a pole built to last and well suited to the task. My carbon pole (a Tri Cast Maestro) is similarly rated and, equipped with the right elastic, I felt that it could do the job.

The terminal rigs that I had seen in action had been fairly simple, although the lack of any shot down the line was something foreign to me on waggler and pole set-ups. The swimfeeder rigs were also a little unusual having a sliding rather than a fixed paternoster link. This, I was told, was because of the danger of the swimfeeder snagging up. The sliding link gave it a chance to pull free rather than cause a breakage.

Bait requirements were also simple. I would take exactly the same as John McCarthy. Ten litres of bait represented a fairly large investment for one match, and it was easy to see why tackle dealers have such an advantage on prolific venues. However, as the match was a mid-week affair, any bait left over could be used on the following weekend and I had to be able to compete with the top men on similar terms. There was always the chance that I might be drawn next to one of them, and to be short of bait represented the kind of disaster that I didn't want to contemplate.

A maverick streak in me toyed with the idea of cereal groundbait, even more so when I was told that it didn't work on the venue and hadn't since the tench catches had ceased. However, although I had seen

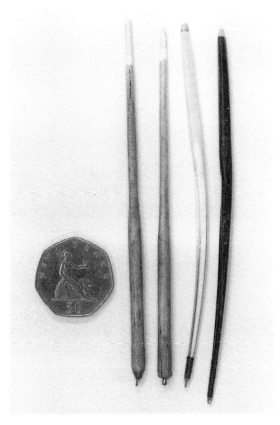

I didn't have an inserted peacock waggler to compare with John McCarthy's close-range float. However, I felt that any one of these would have done a good enough job. The two bent-looking floats are made out of pigeon quills, while the two straight ones are made out of balsa.

one or two anglers with small amounts mixed, I didn't see anyone introduce a substantial amount. If I had decided to groundbait then that was how I would have done it, feeding it positively in the hope that the carp might learn to like it. Special baits such as gozzers or boilies were also dismissed after consulting the experts. I was certainly happier when the latter were crossed off the list. Even to someone as naive as me it seemed like over-complicating matters.

Practice on this venue was an impos-

sibility due to the strict club rulings, so I had to make do with what similar types of fishing I could muster, and a certain trust in experience. I also carefully monitored the progress of the matches on the water to see if any set swims or methods were producing the goods. It quickly became apparent that, as is often the case in a series of matches, one or two anglers figured nearly every time. At Theale, John Larraman was enjoying a phenomenal run – another win and a third placing out of four matches on the venue. Clearly he was in tune with the water.

John McCarthy wasn't far behind though with a second placing and another top six spot confirming his affinity with the water. Significantly, his second placed performance came from an open swim where he was able to employ his fish drawing technique to full advantage. However, another draw on a corner peg saw him frustratingly short of making the prize list.

The cold, wet July of 1988 was not encouraging the carp either, and by the end of the month, catches were well below what had been expected. Strangely enough, on a venue such as this, I felt that I was in with a better chance if the fish did not feed quite so madly as usual. In a catching race, the more polished talents of the top anglers would be certain to leave me adrift, but if the fish did not feed quite so freely, then I would not have quite so much catching up to do.

This had been my experience in the past, especially when I was invited down to a fish catching race supreme at Rye Nook, a gravel pit in Kent. The venue teemed with small rudd and had not been fished seriously for a number of years. Consequently, the fish were in a suicidal mood on the first few occasions when the venue was match fished. An event was arranged with a three-figure match weight as the target.

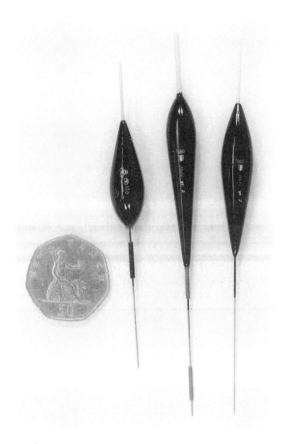

Heavy Irish-style pole floats. The one nearest the coin is of the same pattern that I used at Rye Nook, but at 1.5g, only half the size.

Some of the best known anglers with experience of catching big weights of fish quickly, were invited. Somehow, I managed to sneak an invitation too.

Unlike most of the other competitors, I had no big catches in Ireland to look back on and gain confidence from. This was to be my first attempt at heavy pole fishing. On that day of days I had drawn next to John McCarthy, who was full of enthusiasm and confident that the magic 'ton' would be in his net by the end of the match. For the first hour, he looked to be right, but the fish deserted him for the remainder of the contest. My match took

the opposite route. Obviously, I kept catching that day because the fish had left John and come to me. Why, I don't know, although I had my suspicions.

I fed a very light cloud groundbait throughout the match, and my catch rate only slowed towards the end when I carelessly allowed the feed to become too wet to work properly. The big cloud must have drawn the fish. John, on the other hand, loose fed very heavily and introduced a lot less cereal. During the latter part of the match, he caught two or three decent-sized eels, very close to a kilo apiece. Perhaps the lavish loose feed drew them into the swim. If that was the case, then I am not surprised that the rudd decided to seek pastures new. My swim was handily placed.

I finished the match in seventh place with just over twenty kilos, which turned out to be a good weight from the area that I was in. Because the section did not fish particularly well, I was able to win it. In the section were John McCarthy, Dickie Carr, Ivan Marks and, on the next peg on my left, Kenny Collings. I also have a sneaking suspicion that Bob Nudd might not have been too far away.

The rather laboured point that I am trying to make here is that if the fish had fed as well in that area as they had done on the opposite bank (where the top three weights were 44kg, 27.2kg and 27.1kg), then I would have been buried without trace. There is no doubt in my mind that I would not have been able to stand the pace. I saw how fast John had caught in that first hour. My rate was pedestrian by comparison.

So, I awaited the match with fingers crossed. Naturally I wanted the venue to fish well, but not too well! I was also hopeful of a draw on the big lake. The small one didn't look the sort of place where you could make a mistake and hope to get away with it. The fish circulation was likely to be less than in the more open venue. While I waited for an available ticket, the results declined to the stage where a moderate 14kg was enough for top prize and only 6kg was comfortably into the money. I was hoping for better things than that! Any information that John could muster would obviously be of vital import- ance, and I knew that he would have as good an idea as anybody of the hot methods.

My chance at Theale came at the start of August, which meant that favoured areas were already well established. My chance to draw came when there were just two tickets left. Hoping for a draw on the big lake I got my wish and drew peg 25, the last peg in the hat being number 6, on the small lake.

At least I had got something right, although I wasn't too pleased to learn that I was not on too good an area. My peg was on one of the few deeper spots, in an area called 'the channel', where the lake narrows prior to joining the smaller offshoots. Waggler and feeder were likely to be my most productive methods, but a start, close in on the pole, to see if there were any fish in that area, also looked a good bet.

John Larraman had drawn the peg previously and had caught some big carp in the three kilo range very late in the match. He found these beneath a large overhang- ing bush to his right, and predicted that I would do the same. All in all, it seemed that peg 25 was a swim which offered me a day's fishing, without a great chance of winning any money unless something untoward happened. It was, at least, as it had been described. The neck of the lake, where I was drawn, narrowed to about sixty metres which meant that the middle was well within range of the swimfeeder, with loose feed by catapult at shorter range.

However, my first priority was to set up

a pole rig capable of landing the big carp from under the bush. In order to do this, I had equipped my pole with ultra-heavy 8 Zim elastic, running it through the tele- scopic part as I had done all other grades of elastic on previous occasions. Unfortun- ately, I rather underestimated the strength of this heavy elastic, with the result that I snapped the tip of my pole whilst trying the tension. This was a far from ideal start to the day, but there was a match to be fished, so I tried to forget the incident and concentrated on setting up the waggler and feeder rods.

Harking back to the pole, and as a warn- ing to anyone thinking of emulating my feat, the best way to use excessively heavy elastic is to remove the slender tip section and have the elastic running from the, usually more robust, second section. The cushioning effect of the pole tip is lost, but with elastic of that strength, it is a moot point whether it is worth having anyway.

As I had rather more open water at my disposal than John McCarthy had enjoyed in the first match, I decided to set up a heavier waggler. This was still an inserted peacock quill float, but slightly thicker, to be seen better at distance and carrying a heavier shot load – 3AAA in all. In the approved fashion, I had no shots at all between float and hook, save for a lock shot, and decided to start off fairly heavy with 1.5kg reel line and 1 kg hooklink to a forged 18 hook. The swimfeeder/ledger rig had the same breaking-strain lines, whilst a sliding snap-link swivel allowed me to change quickly between the two ledgering options.

As the waggler and ledger rods were quickly set up, I had enough time to cobble together a makeshift pole rig. For this I used an old glass pole with a very heavy Irish tip, plus the Zim 8 elastic. The pole rig, again on 1.5–1kg lines consisted of a 4 x 15 style pole float with the shots strung

My waggler for Theale. A single long insert in this all peacock quill float took 3 AAA. A compromise between distance, visibility and sensitivity.

down the line shirt-button fashion. As advised, I started the match on this method, alternating my attention between the bush to my right and clear water to my left, fishing four metres to hand. I fed the two near side swims quite heavily with pinkies, whilst catapulting large maggots out to the waggler swim to prepare that area for my next move.

As I expected, the match started with all anglers within my vision feeding at least as heavily as I was. However, I was confident that they might falter at some later stage, allowing my swim to be the only one still enjoying regular, heavy, loose feed, putting me in with a chance of catching fish

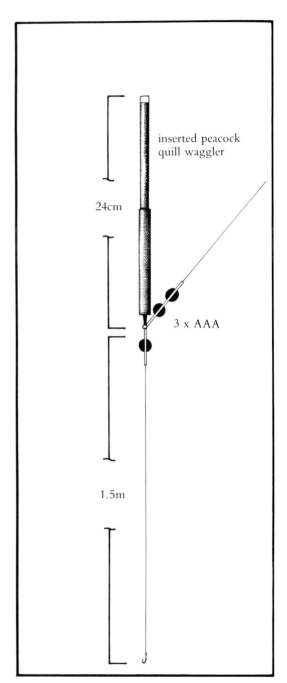

inserted peacock quill waggler

24cm

3 x AAA

1.5m

My waggler rig at Theale.

late in the day. Unfortunately, I did not have a good start to the match. Although my starting method was quite valid, I could not get a bite. Meantime the diverse methods that the anglers around me were using had brought them at least one fish, and in some cases quite a few more.

The anglers opposite, in particular, were catching well, fishing very close in to the features at their disposal. I gained an inkling that I might have drawn on the wrong side for carp. On the other hand, I had been told, in no uncertain fashion, that my swim could well burst into life late in the match, and with the memory of John McCarthy's late charge when I had last watched him, I managed to quell my natural inclination to panic.

Shotting and depth adjustments kept me busy with the near side pole swims for the first half hour or so of the match, but I could not help but notice that the anglers who were still catching seemed to be making no adjustments whatsoever. It gradually dawned on me that there were not very many fish in my swim. Steadily feeding the more distant swim by catapult, I kept my eyes peeled for any signs of surface activity, or of fish taking the maggots on the drop. No signs were forthcoming though, so I continued to prospect the near side, changing hookbaits, depth, shotting, the way I dropped the pole rig into the water and the timing of when I dropped it in (before or after the loose feed). I almost reached the stage where I would have changed sex to have attracted some response!

I decided that half an hour's intensive pole fishing of the two near side swims was more than enough time without so much as a bite, and the waggler offered me a better chance at this stage of the match. However, I continued to feed both inside swims by hand whilst catapulting maggots into the waggler swim. With around a metre and a half to work with, I was able to

keep altering the depth in the hope of attracting a bite on the waggler. Even so sport was worryingly slow. More than an hour had passed and I was still biteless in the true sense of things, although I had seen a couple of line bites on the waggler, one of which came when I was fishing at a depth of around half a metre. Obviously, the fish needed tempting. I decided to slip down a hook size, switching to a size 20 to 0.8kg hooklink. The first priority was to get a fish on the hook, I would worry about landing it later.

In spite of not catching, I did not diminish my feed rate. One of the main reasons for this was John McCarthy's insistence that the feed should be kept going whatever the circumstances. Alternatively, I had a sneaking suspicion that although the anglers near to me had started off by feeding at a similarly heavy rate, they would eventually tail off. Because of this, I was confident that if fish did come into the area late in the match, then it would be me who caught them.

Ninety minutes into the match, I got my first proper bite and landed a fish of around half a kilo without too much trouble. Unfortunately, it was not quite the herald of better times that I had hoped for and another hour passed before I caught my second fish, and identical twin to the first. However, that time did not pass without incident. Keeping up the loose feed even after the float had settled, I attracted a bite which wrenched the rod tip around even before I could drop the catapult and react. Retrieving the tackle I found that the forged hook had been straightened.

Although I concentrated most of my energies on the waggler swim, I had plenty of blank spells in which to prospect the closer areas. Alas, I continued to draw a blank on the inside line, and swimfeeder and ledger tactics on the waggler line also proved fruitless. Thus far in the match, there had been no sign of surface activity from carp within the area of my swim, but I had decided to prepare some floating maggots against this eventuality. I achieved this by popping a handful of maggots into a bait container with just enough water to cover them. Within fifteen minutes, I had enough floating maggots to last me the match and provide me with a bit of variation in bait presentation.

Rather than fish with an all-out floating bait, I decided to try a very slow sinker, putting a floating maggot plus an untreated one, on to the hook. I set the float at around two metres to keep it away from the hookbait, and hopefully allow the semi-buoyant bait to behave in an attractive manner. As I had hoped, this brought an upturn in sport, but not to the extent that I felt in with a chance of winning anything. To add to my problems, I was not landing as many fish as I was getting bites. This was not due to the fish being over large, but because of the way in which they were feeding. The carp did not seem to want to stay in my swim, but instead appeared to cruise through, attracted by the constant rain of loose feed. This meant that they were feeding on the run and bites were correspondingly rapid and unpredictable.

The float would vanish in one motion. Any slack line would tighten in an instant and the rod tip would be wrenched round with alarming vigour as another carp made a hasty exit from the swim. My only answer was to allow rather more slack line than I would have liked though, in hindsight, I may have been better to leave the bale arm open altogether. I was a little unlucky to lose one fish which doubled a maggot over the point of the hook (ever the match angler's problem), whilst another came adrift for no apparent reason. However, I did land one fish of 2kg which put me in a better frame of mind, although

it wasn't quite as big a fish as I had been led to expect. The area under the bush failed to produce a bite throughout, although I gave it every chance.

As I had hoped, sport did pick up towards the latter part of the match, with most activity in the last hour. To emphasise this, one of the anglers opposite, who had enjoyed a very lean time early on, landed over ten kilos of fish in the last hour alone. At the finish, I had had ten bites, hit, or been hit by, eight of them, and had landed just four fish for a weight of 3.5kg.

John's pre-match prediction was that I would get six or seven kilos from the peg, which was a fair estimate taking into account the fish that I had lost. This was one of the biggest differences between myself and the anglers who were well established on the venue. They lost far fewer fish. Experience stood them in good stead, for one of the first things that I learned was that this type of match fishing bore no relation to any that I had done previously. I went to the match with the idea that carp could be treated in the same way as say roach or bream, except that they fought very much harder. This couldn't have been further from the truth. The top men in the field recognised this and were in tune with the fish and the venue. If they had been faced with the kind of bites that I was getting, I am sure that they would have known what to do.

The lack of a practice session on the venue had cost me a few fish I am sure, but, as I had been told at the outset, something spectacular would have had to have happened to see me in with a chance of winning anything. My main mistake was hoping for the fish to feed in a fashion which suited me. The diversity of techniques that I had seen in action on my first visit should have alerted me to the fact that carp fed to suit themselves. However, I had seen enough of Theale in my two visits to

The garage area on the Trent and Mersey Canal at Stretton. Autumn has just started to paint the leaves, a good time of year to draw these particular pegs.

Dickie Carr setting up on the River Lea at Cooks Ferry, one of the grimmest-looking venues I have ever seen.

The view from my peg downstream on the Grand Union Canal at Kings Langley, one of the more scenic canals that I have visited.

Disaster strikes on the Grand Union at Kings Langley – the angler at the next peg downstream from me lands a chub!

Straight into action with a small dace, Sammy's first fish of the day in our practice session. His bulk shotting can be seen clearly in this picture.

Sammy Mann with the fruits of a couple of hours' work on the River Avon. The dismal conditions made us pack up early, but a valuable lesson had been learned.

I must have taken Kenny Collings some good luck when I went walkabout at Theale – as soon as I settled behind him he started to catch.

John Larraman prepares to cast out at Theale.

Contact made, John Larraman hits a bite on the drop.

Safely netted, another carp towards his winning total.

It isn't all bad news on the small lake at Theale. Here an angler prepares to net a lively carp.

Sammy Mann playing a hefty Avon chub. Seconds later the hooklink parted. The spool of nylon that Sammy had used was consigned to the bin.

Kenny Collings had enough confidence in his vintage hooks to give this carp plenty of stick, even though the hook was only a size 22.

Midlands canal ace Simon Nickless on his way to winning another match on the Trent and Mersey Canal. Dickie Carr was keen to pick up a few hints on gudgeon fishing following our match at Kings Langley. He contacted Simon for his advice.

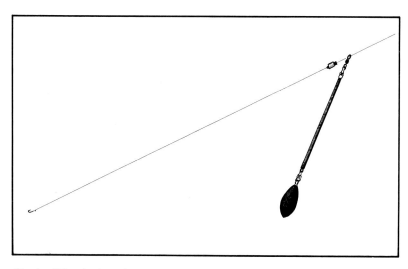

Simple sliding lead rig for carp at Theale.

convince me that it might be worth another go, if I could get tickets for the matches.

Feedwise, I had been interested in the amounts put in by the anglers opposite to me, especially one who had picked up fish throughout the match. His bait bill would have been considerably less than mine, even though he kept up a constant drip of feed into his swim. However, he was fishing at very close range, and it seemed to me that the closer the angler fished the less he had to put in. Also, if the fish were there already, and he had taken one on his first cast, they perhaps didn't need quite so much feed to keep them interested.

Having said that, I had used up all but a litre of bait from the ten litres that I had taken with me. In explanation, this isn't perhaps as much as it sounds. After all, the bait was being spread between three feed areas. Half of the feed was split between the two inside swims, with the other half being pumped into the open water area – in all cases, a reasonable amount of bait for each swim.

What did please me about the match was the fact that the feed method had been right for the waggler swim and, as I expected, I

dominated that area by the end of the match. I was able to attract the bites, I just didn't take all the chances offered. I also managed to beat the angler on either side of me, so perhaps I hadn't failed entirely. Chris Love, John McCarthy's regular travelling companion, pointed out that this should be every angler's first aim. I tried to take some crumb of comfort from those kind words.

What should my catch have been then? Well, I reckon that five kilos would have been a reasonable minimum expectation, but, with the chance of another fish around the two-kilo mark, eight kilos might not have been unreasonable. Even so, it wouldn't have been enough to see me into the prizes, John Larraman failing with nine kilos. The lost fish would have had to average two kilos each to have seen me in with a chance, and I know that they weren't that big!

One other interesting point about the venue was the inconsistent attraction of the various features. In John McCarthy's first peg, the lighter cover held the fish. Too dense a cover, it seemed, did not hold the fish so well. Either that or it was too dense to enable him to put his bait where the fish actually were, meaning that he had to lure them out from their hiding place.

There were no hard and fast rules though. Cover of some sort was a bonus, but it did not mean that the fish would be there for the duration of the match, rather they might visit it sometime.

Reed beds appeared to be quite good news, but again, not all of them seemed to hold quite the same attraction. A reasonable depth close to the reeds was a requirement for the fish to feel secure.

Having drawn peg 25, I was able to take a look at the much vaunted peg 28 after the match. In spite of the fact that it was positioned on a slight point, it looked otherwise quite unremarkable. It had produced the goods again, though, with another catch into double figures of kilos. What I couldn't see were the underwater features, and it may be that these have a bearing on the distribution of carp at Theale (and any other venue). Certainly, what appeared to be low water levels, in spite of the wet summer, seemed to have shifted the fish from some of the swims that John expected to produce. However, his style of fishing for them meant that he was always in with a chance of picking up fish on the move from one area to another.

The interesting thing about the two lakes at Theale was the way in which John approached them, although I did not find this out until after my match. On the smaller venue, John's favoured technique was to lay a bed of feed and wait for the fish to find it rather than showering it in throughout, as he tended to do on the large lake. He had found this to be the best method for him on the small lake, although he was at a loss to explain exactly how the method worked, or why the blitz-feed method did not. However, on the larger lake, he was more interested in attracting the fish into his swim if they were not there at the start. On the smaller lake he felt that

angling disturbance tended to move the fish around and he was mainly interested in keeping them there for as long as possible once they had arrived. Perhaps the disturbance of loose feed falling amongst them would have hastened them on their way.

Theale was certainly a different kind of venue to the ones that I had been used to, but it was a kind of fishing that I thought I might be able to get used to, given a bit more time. One thing that did cross my mind was how the anglers would cope when the carp put on a bit more muscle and became more of a handful. Match tactics revolving around fine lines would still be needed to attract a bite, as that is what the fish would be used to, however, adherence to such methods inevitably brings its own problems where carp are concerned. The carp at Theale had given me the run-around and I hadn't hooked any of the bigger fish which inhabit the place.

Looking to the future of these venues, I do think that there might be a few match wins waiting for the angler who adopts, or adapts, some of the specimen hunting rigs. The hair rig looks most promising if it can fool the carp into thinking that the bait is being presented on very fine line, when in reality the hook is attached to 3 or 4kg nylon. However, I am not so sure if the match angler's 'catch anything' style would be easily married to such a rig, especially as baiting up would take longer and the range of methods used would perhaps diminish. Float fishing, for example, might be more difficult.

What is certain is that if there is any thinking to be done on the specimen X match methods, then it will come from the Southern anglers who have already made their mark with this sort of match fishing. I, for one, will be looking at the summer match results with a keen interest, especially at Theale!

6 What Did I Learn?

Watching four very different anglers on a good cross-section of venues was an edifying experience. To start with, and as I suspected, there was nothing which immediately struck me as being very different. However, it must be said that I did not always see them under the best of circumstances, and a far longer spying mission was really required.

However, the quartet had some things in common which I noticed were missing from the other anglers that I sat behind. The most obvious one was self-belief. They never doubted for one moment that they might be in with a chance of winning something. Because of this, there was no sign of panic as their matches drew to a close, and the final whistles saw them concentrating as hard as at the all-in.

When they hooked big fish they expected to land them, and played them with a calm assurance. Nigel Bull's peformance with his match-winning chub was exemplary, and watching him playing it took my mind back to a couple of years earlier and the Division One National on the Oxford Canal. There, I had hooked a decent chub on a similar fine hooklink and tiny hook, although I was using a rod and line at the time. The chub ran right under a small bush that was giving my peg some cover, and, because of the frail hooklink, I had to let it run. However I didn't feel confident of landing it. Not surprisingly, the chub found a snag and sheared through the slender line.

Although that chub was probably only half the size of Nigel's, it would have boosted my team to around sixth place. I think that Nigel might have got it out. Nigel's patience when playing his match-winning fish was astonishing, and was a major factor in landing it. Because he did not try to hustle it to the net the first time that it came within range, he did not panic it into a frenzied, tackle-smashing dash. The fish was tired in the way that a marathon runner is tired and had nothing left for a sprint finish.

Another thing that struck me about Nigel's two performances was his very busy style. I taped our conversation on the first match at Stretton and although it was a windy day the sound was not too bad. However, there was an almost constant noise on the tape that was driving me mad until I realised what it was. A very high-pitched sawing sound is the best way of describing it. It was a roach pole being shuffled back and forth across the canal.

Seeing and doing are two different things though, and the effort involved in shipping the pole back and forth makes it a tempting prospect to wait for a proper bite to develop or to lift the pole sufficiently high so that the bait can be examined prior to dropping it back into the swim. Neither method is satisfactory, but an angler would need a will of iron not to succumb to the temptation to be lazy.

The one area of worry is the amount of time wasted by the constant movement of the pole, the bait hardly having time to fish properly before it is moved around.

However, when the bites start to come to this method, time and motion are all important and with bites coming quickly, the tackle has to be manipulated with similar speed and dexterity. Apart from that, Nigel feels sure that he is fishing as efficiently as possible. He knows that his bait will be more likely to attract a swift response because it has not been torn to pieces. He is not trying to attract a bite with a bloodworm skin on his hook, or his hookbait covered with detritus. He is not wasting time by repeatedly bringing back his pole, he is saving it.

The amount of practice that Nigel has put in pays off in other areas too. Weather conditions can have quite an effect on canal results as they can change the feeding patterns of different species of fish. By practising under a variety of conditions the angler is able to have a good guess at what might work on any given day. This means that time can be saved by adopting the correct tactic straight away, making the match less of a gamble.

Even in my limited experience, I have noticed certain patterns develop – a heavy frost will tend to slow down canal sport, especially if it is the first one following a mild spell – but Nigel has more idea of which tactics would work under those circumstances than I do. I only know that if a sudden thaw takes place after a canal has been covered in ice for a few days, then roach will be quite likely to feed. Rather less keen will be gudgeon, so I wouldn't waste too much time going for them.

As the Trent and Mersey is Nigel's local canal, he is in tune with its special cycles with regard to the balance of species in the venue. For the past few seasons, roach have played an ever more dominant role in the results on the canal. I thought that this was because more people were fishing for them, but the answer is not quite as simple as that.

Less anglers are fishing for gudgeon because there are a lot less of them about than there were five or six years ago. They are certainly not evenly spread along the canal, tending to be isolated in certain areas. However, it does seem to be worthwhile giving the inside line a try just in case there is a pocket of them in the vicinity. An easily caught kilo is not to be sniffed at on any canal. Nigel had noticed what appeared to be a new generation of gudgeon figuring in his catches this year but, at a couple of centimetres long, they are a pest at the moment and to be avoided if possible. In a few years time, though, it might become a winning proposition to go for the gudgeon on the short line again.

John McCarthy was very forthright in his summing-up. His knowledge of the southern carp scene is phenomenal and he appears to have all of the relevant information neatly indexed in some mental filing cabinet. John's main aim is to take any angling style down to its basics – the simpler the better, as far as he is concerned. That is not to say that he is inflexible, far from it, but he does have the knack of sorting out the most productive aspects of any particular technique and discarding those that are superfluous and time wasting.

John mainly concerns himself with how to catch as many carp from his swim in the least possible time, even down to the manner in which he plays his fish. The specimen hunters' side strain technique, for instance, does not enter into John's armoury. He holds his rod as near to vertical as possible, putting the full shock absorbing bend of the rod into play. It tires the carp very quickly. Another area where John's 'lowest common denominator' method seems to work is in his choice of baits. On our first match, I was amazed by the variety of different baits that some anglers had taken with them. John's view was that somewhere in the lakes were carp

John McCarthy putting maximum pressure on to one of Theale's hard fighting carp.
Keeping the rod high tires the fish more quickly.

that were hungry for maggots, and there was a good chance that he would attract them.

I am pretty certain that had I not seen John in action on the first match, I would have caught far fewer fish, or at least attracted far fewer bites, when I fished the pits myself. Most of the anglers that I could see appeared to have resident shoals of fish corralled up by some feature. They might have struggled if they had been forced to fish into open water.

The carp fishing episode had another kickback in showing just how late a catching period can be left if the fish are of sufficient size. Say an angler required twenty carp to win – that is only four fish per hour. But he would be unlikely to catch them at such an even pace and more probable would be a last two-hour run at ten an hour – pretty hectic sport with carp. However, the same applies to any of the big species with which match anglers are concerned. The angler does not have to be picking up chub, bream, barbel or tench every few seconds. A blank hour or two, whilst not desirable, is no disaster.

Patience has never been my strong point, and I am sure that it is not John's either, but he has mastered his impetuosity and the lesson was well learned. Although John played his carp very hard he was also very careful, treating each fish as though it might be his last. Because of this, he lost very few through fragile hookholds tearing free, the main casualties coming as a result

Confidence in bait is vital. John McCarthy was certain that his was the best available, and there was plenty of it. This was just a small sample.

of the maggot doubling over the point of the hook. This was a feature of all of these anglers. They lost very few fish, and were genuinely surprised if one came off the hook or escaped by some other means.

Dickie Carr, for instance, was amazed when his match-winning chance waved goodbye on the Lea at Cooks Ferry. I wouldn't have felt in with any sort of chance of landing that fish before I had seen some of these anglers in action. Another common feature was that they were never satisfied. The most extreme example was Nigel Bull and his flying pole technique, but all of them had aspirations to perfection.

With John, this manifested itself in his attention to detail with his bait. Naturally, as a tackle dealer, he has a distinct advantage. However, I sometimes feel that this is a very neglected area. Nigel too was fussy with regard to his bloodworm and joker supplies, preferring to scrape his own rather than rely on the whims of a commercial source. This certainly paid dividends on the Bank Holiday Monday match when he must have been one of the few anglers on the bank with a very fresh supply of bait, most others having to settle for some very sad looking bloodworm and joker.

Dickie Carr's minute adjustments to his pole rig in readiness for the Cooks Ferry match were also quite important. I am sure that too many anglers fish with their bloodworm dragging on the bottom because they fish a few inches over depth. This is often not the best way to fish it, the ideal situation being having just the very tail of the worm lightly brushing the bottom, meaning that the hook itself may be around a centimetre under depth. Shortening a pre-prepared rig was something a lot of anglers, myself included, would only have done during the match if at all, but Dickie had the foresight to do it before the match commenced, which meant that he had

perfect presentation from the word go. Attention to detail naturally encompasses many of the smaller items such as micro shots and hooks. Again, Dickie was very particular, although he had a definite rival in Sammy Mann.

Not only had Sammy's hooklink nylon to be of a certain preferred brand, it also had to be the correct colour. Even then he was justifiably suspicious of any shortcomings. On our practice day, what was obviously a very hefty chub inexplicably cracked Sammy's hooklink off when he was exerting very little pressure. I wasn't quite prepared for how apologetic Sammy would be following such an incident. He felt that I had witnessed an extremely poor piece of angling. Not only that, but when we returned to the caravan, the offending spool of nylon from which he had tied his hooklink was instantly consigned to the rubbish bin. It was given no second chance.

Hooks were largely a matter of personal choice amongst these men, but as an interesting side-issue, when I was talking to Kenny Collings on the first Theale trip, I discovered that he was using some of the original Mustad 90340 barbless size 22 hooks, that is, the ones that came in tiny paper boxes. For some reason, once Mustad went to the plastic boxes, some of their hooks, particularly the 90340, went downhill. Every angler using them at the time (and there were a lot of us), noticed the change. The points blunted quickly and the hooks were more prone to opening out. Typically, Kenny had come across a supply via bankrupt stock of another tackle outlet. He said that they were not for sale in his shop!

Dickie Carr was particularly impressed with the Italian Tubertini hooks, so much so that he was even willing to use them as ready-made hooks to nylon – something that very few of the top anglers are willing to do. Obviously, as I mentioned earlier, he shortened the hook length in the lower breaking strains to the extent that he did not need to put split shot on to it, but the hooks themselves certainly looked very good.

On the pole, the microbarb hook was the universal choice, whatever pattern. Not too well publicised, but something of an open secret now, the microbarb prevents very tiny fish from falling off the hook as the pole is being shipped back in. Slack line used to allow a lot of small fish to drop off of barbless hooks, the weight and strength of the fish being insufficient to keep the line tight. I found another use for microbarbs, but more of that later.

For others (not everyone has hoarded a few 90340s away like Kenny Collings), it was a case of the strongest, lightest forged hook available. Unfortunately, most of these tend to be barbed hooks, but the barbs were flattened down with a pair of electrician's pliers.

It might be old-fashioned, but these anglers tend to use at least one size smaller hook for any given application than the majority of match anglers. I mentioned Kenny Collings and his size 22s to John McCarthy and John Larraman. John Larraman said 'I think old Kenny might have something there,' in a casual throw-away manner. At the next match, the two Johns went to the size 22 very early! Similarly, Sammy Mann had no qualms about fishing casters on a size 22, although he did make one concession and leave the point showing. I thought back to the years when I had used size 22 hooks before they were fashionable. I beat Stan Smith at the next peg on the north bank of the Nene around the time of the first Division One National on the venue using size 22 hooks to catch a few nice skimmers. I don't use them so often now.

Nigel Bull also fished both hemp and casters on the same size 24 hook that he used for bloodworm. I have always found hemp bites on the canal hard enough to hit on a size 20, and I know plenty of anglers who fish it on a size 18 if they can get away with it. It is all food for thought though. A lot of anglers, and I count myself amongst them, only use the very small hooks during matches. Practice sessions are usually conducted using at least a size 20. How, then, can we expect to be confident of landing that big bonus fish on a size 22 or 24, if the only time we use them is in a match environment with our adrenalin already pumping? The answer is, we can't.

I don't like using tiny hooks unless I have to because I think that it does fishing more harm than good in the long term. To compete at that level, however, I think that you have to use such tackle as a matter of course, just to get used to using it. Funnily enough, when I fished the Burton Joyce open matches, the size 22 hook was an accepted starting point, but, not too many fish were lost because of it. However, on the upper Trent, near to my home, it used to be a real struggle to keep fish on the hook when using a size 22. The only difference that I can think of, is the average depth. Perhaps fish stick to the hook better in an average depth of two-and-a-half metres than they do in one-and-a-half metres.

I have already mentioned Nigel Bull being in tune with his local canal and this was no less evident in the other anglers. In one of the last matches in the Theale series, John McCarthy fished the straight ledger in preference to his normal all-action float style. He did very well because he was one of the few anglers to realise that bites would be at a premium following a drop in temperature. Surely everyone must have noticed that, but how many did anything about it? Sammy Mann recognised the signs that he associated with the start of the chub season on the Warwickshire Avon.

He was unable to do anything about it on our match together, but he would have had a very real advantage if he had drawn in the right area.

Not everyone was perfect, however, and Dickie Carr did make a mistake on the canal at Kings Langley, but he vowed to do something about it. Before the weekend was out he had spent a few hours on the telephone to another Midlands canal ace, Simon Nickless, picking up a few tips on the finer points of gudgeon fishing. These anglers are far from machines, and they do recognise when they have made mistakes. However, they do have a habit of getting it right more often than the vast majority of anglers.

What about the pegs that they drew? Well, the number of times that I was able to watch them was scarcely representative of a whole season, but, as should have been self-evident, they did not draw too many fliers. However, they did not suffer too many no-hopers either. John McCarthy fished the entire series at Theale (apart from one match when he was in Ireland), and only drew out of the big lake on one occasion.

Nigel Bull really did make something happen on what was a very strange peg, however. The following open on the Horninglow section saw the angler that drew it not bothering to fish it. While the peg is not that bad, it is also not held in

Looks familiar? Tony Scott brings a fish to hand on the canal at Stretton on his way to second place in the match. Nigel Bull had a similar weight when he drew the peg, but on that day it wasn't worth a bean.

especially high regard by some of the local matchmen who think that they know the water a little too well. As a bit of a sting in the tail, Tony Scott drew Nigel's Hillfield Lane peg from our first match at Stretton, on a very frost-affected day and took second place, only ten grams behind the winner! On that day, the normally favoured garage section fished like an ice-box as the tree cover is so lavish that it prevented the sun from warming the water. I suppose, in fairness, you can be in with some sort of chance anywhere on a canal, especially if you have Nigel's or Tony's ability.

On the drawing front, once you get to the standard of ability that these anglers have reached, it is no longer necessary to draw a flier every time. Avoiding the no-hopers is important though, because, as I said earlier, there are some areas that you just cannot win from, no matter what standard you are.

7 How Did It Affect Me?

It would be nice to say that, thanks to the influence of these four anglers, I started winning nearly every match I fished. To avoid keeping you in suspense, I will tell you now that this was not the case. However, watching, and talking to these anglers did make some difference to my results.

I had an inkling that the pole was going to play a significant role in my ventures abroad, so I decided to fish a few matches on a venue suited to it. I chose a small, but deep, ballast pit near to my home, and the first match on the first weekend of the season. An early start, and just as well because summer was at its height in early June.

I drew a fairly nondescript peg on the roadside bank of the pit, in spite of having a fancy for the opposite side. However, I had drawn correctly as it later turned out. I decided to fish eight metres to hand as the pit drops off to between four and five metres deep only a short distance from the bank, with a one-and-a-half to two-metre-deep shelf stretching some two metres from the bank. Because I was aiming to catch small roach and skimmers, I decided to fish in the continental style and put in an initial heavy feed of groundbait laced with squatts about six metres from the bank.

I decided to experiment and used two fairly active Van Den Eynde groundbaits – 75 per cent Kastaar to 25 per cent Beet. I was pleased to see that the blurb on the booklet was not exaggerating as it remained active for quite some time. My float rig was fairly simple and I aimed to catch the bulk of my fish in the last metre of water. I certainly did not want them to come up and take on the drop, as in the past this has resulted in a lot of missed bites and bumped fish. I also felt that by fishing the full depth I would be in with a better chance of a bonus tench or bream.

The float that I used was one of the Milo range particularly suited to stillwaters being of virtual antenna shape. The pattern is called Isis. I shotted it with one SSSG and one BB on a length of fine silicon tubing, rather than a normal olivette, and had one number 12 micro as a dropper below this. Initially, I set the bulk one metre from the hook, with the drop shot midway between the bulk and the hook. As it was an early-season match, I did not expect the fish to be too sophisticated, and a size 20 hook to 0.70kg line completed the rig.

The match started perfectly and a succession of small roach and skimmer bream came to my single gozzer hookbait. The only slight problem that I had was that I bumped the odd fish as I lifted into them, possibly because I was using rather stronger elastic than was ideal for the size of fish that I was catching. The bites were coming regularly but they weren't coming particularly quickly. However, by the end of the first hour, I estimated that I had around a kilo of small fish in my net. Around the hour mark, I boosted my catch with a skimmer of half a kilo, but it proved to be a lone fish about ten times the size of the stamp that I was catching most regularly.

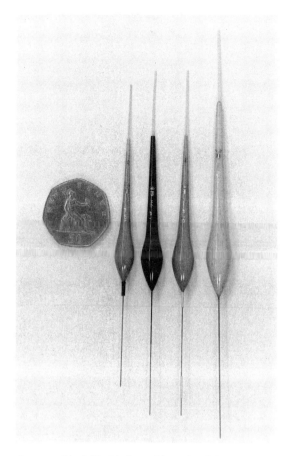

A range of the Milo Isis floats. I have found them to be brilliant on stillwaters, especially for working the bait Dickie Carr-style. Another plus is that the top eye is set quite low on these floats, which makes them a good choice for wind-whipped canals during the winter months. However, they are next to useless during the summer or on venues like the Oxford Canal where boat traffic creates excessive flow.

I had decided at the outset to fish the pole all the way through but, by the half-way mark, bites were starting to tail off and I decided that it might be worth while setting up an alternative. Accordingly, I attempted to set up an open-ended swim-feeder rig on my quivertip rod, whilst letting the pole tackle fish for itself. This was a mistake. Not only did I miss ten or a

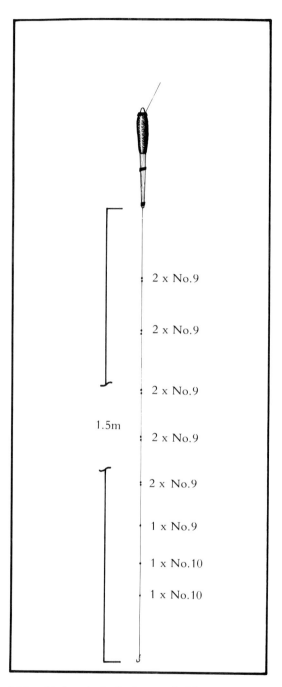

2 x No.9

2 x No.9

2 x No.9

1.5m   2 x No.9

2 x No.9

1 x No.9

1 x No.10

1 x No.10

Light stick float rig for the first round of the summer league. I stayed on it too long.

dozen bites whilst setting the other rod up, it took me twice as long because I was not concentrating on the job in hand. When I eventually tried the swimfeeder, I was disappointed to find the same stamp of fish that I had been catching on the pole. The swimfeeder was far too slow a method for these fish, so I reverted to my original line of attack.

The angler at the next peg would not let me settle and for the remainder of the match, it seemed that every time I had a quiet spell he would pick up a decent fish on the feeder. Naturally, this prompted me to give it another time-wasting try just on

the off chance of a bonus fish. It never came, and the blank spells cost me dearly as I finished second in the match with 4kg 187g, beaten by 50g. I thought of the bites that I had missed on the pole while I had been setting the lead rod up. My quartet of anglers did not make this kind of error.

My next match on the venue followed my first meetings with Dickie Carr and John McCarthy. This time I drew a peg at one of the ends of the rectangular lake, luckily the end into which the wind was blowing. Again, I only set up the pole, but this time I fed two distinct swims – one with groundbait and squatts, the other

I was soaked through, on a grim peg, and every time I hooked a decent fish, it knocked itself off against some piece of floating weed. No wonder I didn't seem to enthusiastic about this match on the River Trent.

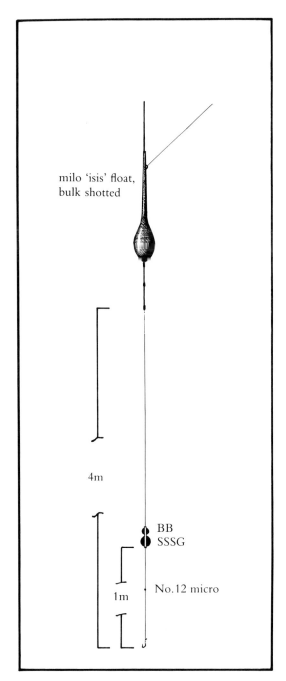

milo 'isis' float,
bulk shotted

4m

BB
SSSG

No.12 micro

1m

My ballast pit pole rig.

with loose casters for roach. I caught off both sets of feed, with the groundbait proving superior. However, the average size of the fish on the caster line was somewhat larger. At the half-way point, both swims died, and it was only in the last half hour of the match that I began to pick up odd fish again. However, I managed just short of three kilos for fifth place, with every catch ahead of me containing a bonus fish or two. I filed the caster ploy away for future reference. One point that had struck home after watching Dickie Carr was the vaseline trick. In the facing wind, it made all the difference between fishing properly and not.

A team match on the River Trent saw me drawn in a desperate area that, on past form, I would be sure to struggle on. Floating weed was a real menace for most of the match, and because of it I was only able to land one fish of over a hundred grams. The rest – all small chub – seemed to have no problem in transferring the hook to a handy piece of the green floating matter. It was here that I found the micro-barb hooks to be useful as they did, at least, keep the smaller fish on the hook.

I made a couple of mistakes in this match. One was not setting a waggler rod up. There were anglers on the opposite bank and this dissuaded me. However, I am sure that I would have picked up a few better fish. The weed would have been an even bigger problem then, though. My second mistake was to continue to feed the swim too lightly. I was catching very tiny fish all day and only stepped up the feed late on to see what would happen. I then began to pick up a slightly better stamp of chub, but again, they were a problem to get out. I finished the match with around a kilo and a half and below tenth in the section – not an ideal start to the series.

Back to the stillwater and I drew a peg two spots along from my opening second

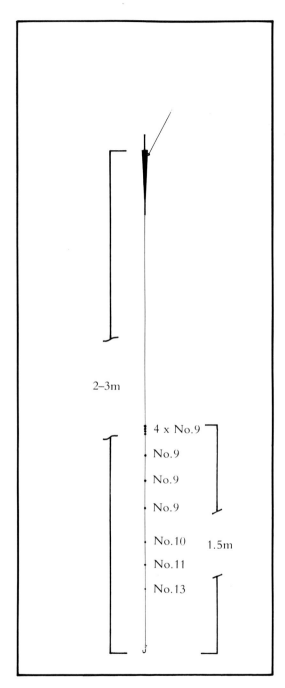

2–3m

4 x No.9

No.9

No.9

No.9

No.10

1.5m

No.11

No.13

0.50g pole rig set up for caster fishing on the first shelf of the ballast pit.

I do buy some of my floats. These very light sticks have served me well on the River Trent. I opted for one of these in the opening round of the summer league.

placing. Again, it was the standard pole rig, but this time I set up an additional one on the spare tip section, specifically for fishing caster on the top shelf. I also set up a ledger rod in preparation for any blank spells. I would not be caught napping again.

As usual, I started with five big balls of groundbait laced with squatts on the six metre line, whilst feeding casters and hemp well to my left on top of the shelf. I started on the groundbait line as I expected instant results from this area. I was right, but the fish were very slow in coming and I felt that I was not really catching quickly enough. However, I persevered for an hour to give the caster swim time to mature. This was to be my main back up and I did not want to catch fish from it too soon in case I unsettled them.

When, at last, I did go for them, they were ready and waiting, and a reasonable stamp of roach. I was also expecting the odd bonus tench or two on this method. In fact, I got one, but at only a third of a kilo it was not quite the bonus that I had hoped for. Surprisingly, I caught more skimmers than roach from the caster swim, although I had to use it more often than I would have liked because the groundbait and maggot swim had produced rather poorly.

A few casts on the open-ended feeder picked me up a handful of small skimmers which kept me ticking over nicely. From my peg I could see that not much of note was being caught, although the angler on my right had picked up a few nice fish, and also lost a couple. It seemed that whenever he changed to a different method, he would hook a fish in the half-kilo class. Mine were much smaller and I was certain that I was well behind him.

With about half an hour left, I decided on a concerted effort on the swimfeeder, and put in six cricket-ball-sized helpings of groundbait in readiness. Letting this settle for a few minutes, I tried both pole lines, picking up another couple of hand-sized skimmers on the caster in quick succession. I stayed with that method for longer than I intended. With only ten minutes to go, the angler on my right struck into a fish on the swimfeeder, inevitably a half-kilo special. Not to be beaten, I decided on a last gamble.

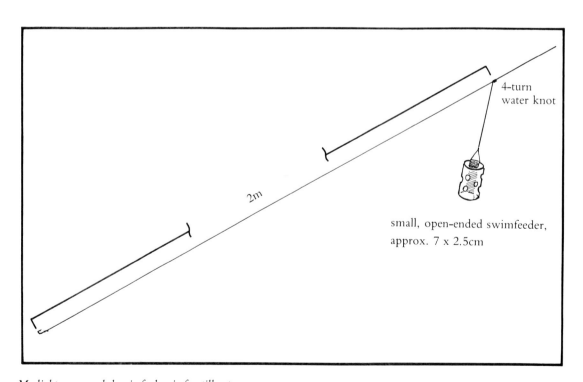

4-turn water knot

2m

small, open-ended swimfeeder, approx. 7 x 2.5cm

My light, open-ended swimfeeder rig for stillwaters.

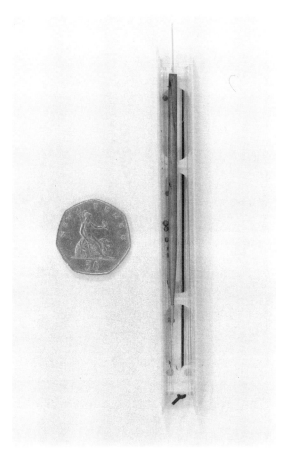

This is the caster rig that I set up for my stillwater match.

With only four minutes remaining, the tip pulled round in a lovely slow bite and I bumped into what was obviously a decent fish. I played it carefully in with no alarms and duly netted it with a couple of minutes remaining. At a kilo and a half it was the sort of bonus that I had been looking for, another one would put me in with a chance. I rapidly rebaited, refilled the feeder and with a piece of rare luck dropped it right on to the correct spot. I willed the tip to pull round again, but the all out sounded before I had another chance.

The angler that had been giving me trouble all match was on the scales and weighed in my fish first. On the strength of the big bonus skimmer, I weighed in 2kg 292g – not a great total. Next door, the angler was unlucky to come up just short with 2kg 264g (the lost fish had cost him). Luckily for me, the lake had fished very poorly and I managed to hang on for a win thanks to that last, lucky fish.

Going back to the six balls of groundbait, I realised that that amount of feed is not usual on most bream venues. Indeed, I rarely feed like that and am usually as cautious as the next man. However, with nearly five metres of water to play with I decided to be bold with the feed, and luckily it worked. Nevertheless, I think that the shoal of bream were just moving through when I dropped on them.

The second round of our local summer league put me on to a section that holds a few bream. Although this section spreads over more than a thousand metres of river, I always seem to draw in the same 100-metre area, and one that is not too well known for its bream potential. The day of the match saw the river still carrying a few inches of extra water – not enough to prevent me from fishing the waggler but enough to make it less effective than normal.

I started off with bream in mind, and decided to feed groundbait quite heavily at about thirty-five metres. I didn't really fancy my chances of catching much on the stick float so I didn't bother to set one up. I would be unlikely to catch more than a kilo on that method and that would not be any good in the section that I had drawn. My main methods were to be the waggler and open-ended swimfeeder.

In recent seasons, the best ploy for bream in this section of the river has been an initial heavy production of feed, topped up with smaller helpings throughout the match. I therefore opened up with ten cricket-ball-sized helpings of groundbait –

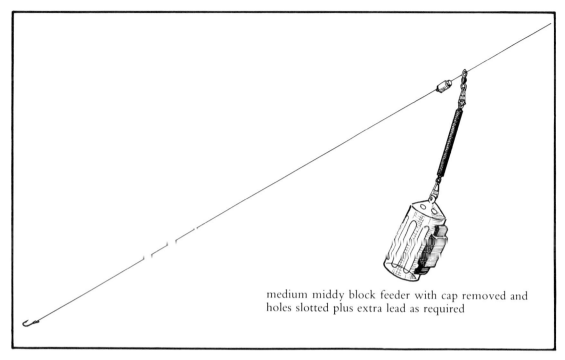

medium middy block feeder with cap removed and holes slotted plus extra lead as required

My groundbait feeder rig for the upper Trent – simple but effective.

four directly in front, three more on the same line but slightly downstream and the final three, straight out in front again but about five metres further out than the original feed. This was a saving ploy in case the bream decided to drift downstream and further out as the match progressed. The further groundbait might keep them in the swim for a while longer, and there was a chance that they might move back on to the main area later.

My groundbait mix was mainly brown crumb, but with the addition of half a bag of Van Den Eynde Beet and quarter of a bag of Van Den Eynde Kanal. This makes a fairly heavy mix which is a necessity in the pacy waters of the River Trent. I intended to add a touch of brasem to the main feed later in the match, but not at the outset. The reason for this is that I think its added aroma can sometimes attract bream to the swimfeeder because it stands out

from the feed already introduced. By putting brasem into the base mix this advantage is lost. Certainly, when I have tried it in the past, bites have increased in both frequency and therefore number.

The quantity of groundbait that I mixed at the start had a dry weight of around three kilos and contained a couple of litres of additional feed items. This was made up of a litre of casters, put into the base mix, and a litre of squatts, put in as required. The squatts were equally portioned white and red, in two separate containers and were riddled from the sand before adding to the mix. I used the different colours in deference to the bream's penchant for different colours at different times. It gave me another choice of bait should I not be catching.

My main bait for loose feeding was three litres of white maggots, with a few reds sprinkled amongst them, and I also had a

I was expecting to pick up a few skimmers of this size in the second round of the summer league, and fed the swim accordingly. This time, though, it very nearly backfired.

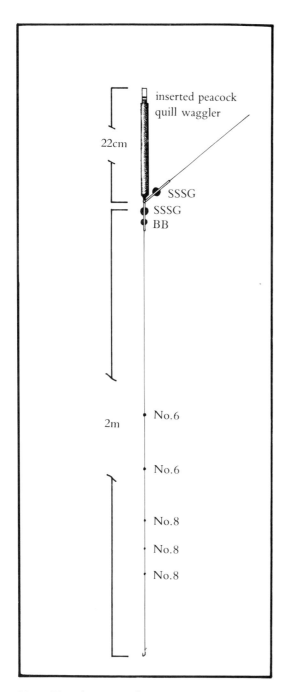

Upper Trent bream waggler rig.

good supply of redworms, having done well with them in the past. I started the match with a two-and-a-half SSSG waggler, locked with 2 SSSG and a BB, with a further two sixes and two eights spread down the line. This is more lead down than I normally use on the River Trent, but I wanted to be sure that the bait dragged well along the bottom. A few trial casts with the float set at two and a half metres revealed that the bottom shot, half a metre from the hook, was dragging bottom. However, it did not appear to be slowing the float down quite enough so I added another size 8 about three centimetres below this. Now the float travelled through the swim in a way that I liked, but would it be equally attractive to the bream?

Bites proved to be scarce, although I had expected a few silver fish to start with before the bream decided to feed. By persevering I picked up a couple of small roach, a dace and a chub, plus the inevitable gudgeon, but after an hour I still had less than half a kilo in the net. Half an hour on the swimfeeder proved no better, and in spite of putting the odd egg-sized ball of groundbait in to top up my first feed, the bream that I was sure were there would not be tempted.

The two anglers upstream of me were catching steadily on an inside line, one on the stick float and running line, the other on seven metres of pole. I still didn't think that they would catch throughout on these methods, but by now they had built up a substantial lead. I resisted the temptation to follow them on to the inside line for a couple of reasons. One was that I was certain that I would pick up a few bream so long as I kept at them and didn't mess about. The other was that only one such fish would be needed to make good the early damage.

With an hour and a half gone, the angler downstream of me really rubbed salt into

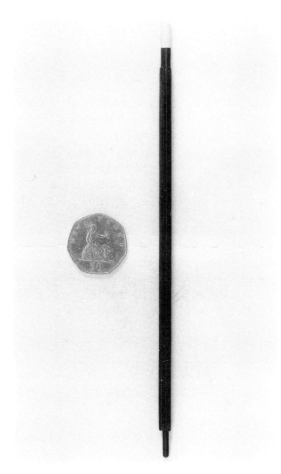

This peacock quill float has a slightly stepped insert allowing a fair show of float while retaining sensitivity. I use it as an all-round float, when I am fishing mainly for bream on the upper Trent, but also want to catch anything else that is going.

the wounds by taking a bream with his first cast on the swimfeeder, the fish apparently taking on the drop as I saw the rod nearly wrenched from his hands. However, I had decided on another go on the waggler and stuck to it, though by now I was attracting very few bites on the method. I decided to top up my feed with a further four cricket balls – three on the main line and one further – in an effort to draw the fish away from the angler downstream.

Within half an hour, the downstream angler had latched into another couple of bream, unfortunately (for him), losing one at the net. I began to wonder if the fish would move up to me and the bed of feed that I had laid in readiness. With half of the match now gone, I was well behind the catch rate of my immediate neighbours, although I still expected to be able to pull something out of the fire if my previous experiences on the section had been anything to go by.

The previous season I had taken four skimmers in a hectic fifteen minutes to snatch an advantage over Robin Banton on the next peg upstream, weighing in somewhere around three and a half kilos for good section points. Prior to that, I had gone from around last in the section to second, on the strength of a bream that weighed just under two and a half kilos on its own, that I landed with less than three minutes of the match remaining. I had about eighty grams of other fish to go with it.

I also knew that if I was struggling to catch on the waggler so were the other anglers, and indeed, bank walkers suggested that not much was being caught. Under these circumstances, the feeder was the best option so it was at this stage that I added about a tablespoonful of brasem to what remained of my feed. That may seem a small amount, but I have found that this very strong additive can put bream off if too much is used. If I can smell it in a mix of groundbait I think that there is too much. However, that was the key that I hoped would unlock a couple of bream and boost me to respectability.

I also decided to make one of the few adjustments open to the swimfeeder angler, and altered the length of the tail between the feeder and the hook, lengthening it to almost two metres. This did the trick, just as I was talking to Derby's Mark Warren, who was bank running for the

Measham tackle dealer, Robin Banton, with a brace of nice chub. He could have done with those in the summer league match where I had a quick run of skimmers to just pip him.

Roachpole Team. I felt rather than saw, the feeder rod give a characteristic nod and perfect drop back that signalled a bream bite. I tightened into the slack line and felt the satisfying thump of a half-kilo skimmer – another victim of the trusty redworm, a brilliant scratching bait for bream on the Trent. The fish gave me no trouble on a size 18 feeder hook to 1kg hooklink and, with a feeling of relief, I slipped it into the keepnet.

Thirty minutes later, I repeated the dose. There was still an hour and a half to go – plenty of time for a few more. By now, almost every angler in the vicinity had switched to the feeder, apart from the angler upstream of me who stuck manfully to the waggler. Given the choice, he too would have been swimfeeding, but he had not brought his feeder rod with him. However, he did manage a skimmer on the waggler.

It was obvious that the angler down-stream of me was right on top of the shoal of bream as he continued to attract bites. A couple of lost fish unsettled them though, and when he cracked off his swimfeeder whilst casting out, his re-tackling gave me the opportunity to roll a straight ledger as close to his catching area as I dared. Unfor-tunately, it was without result. He had scarcely fed his swim at all, so I continued to feed my swim heavily in an attempt to draw the fish away from him. I wonder why I didn't get the message that this was the wrong thing to do until I was mulling the day's results over in the bar after the match.

Fifteen minutes from the end, I boosted my catch with a nice fish that took me to just over two and a half kilos. At the end, the angler downstream had beaten me comfortably with 3.5kg, taking two bream more than I managed by feeding about two kilos of groundbait less. However, at least I was able to return with top six section points and the team moved up a few places in the league.

The final match on the lake saw me drawing what I thought was a good peg, on the point, directly opposite to the scene of my win. With a long cast on the swim-feeder I could almost fish the same spot. The area had also produced the winner on the second match so I felt confident of being in with a chance. It appeared that the area had not been fishing well in the weeks just prior to the match, but I had a feeling that I might be able to do something.

The advantage of pegs in that area is that fish, moving around the lake, are sure to pass them, and I was rapidly forming the opinion that the bigger fish in the venue tended to do a lot of roaming. With this in mind, the small fish that I was going to base the bulk of my attack on would not be so important if they were absent. However, I did feel that they might be less of a gamble than the bigger bream.

Again, I set up two poles and a feeder rod, though, in the strong left to right wind, the poles would take a bit of handling. My groundbait for this match was slightly different, although it was not of my making. I discovered that the Kastaar Van Den Eynde groundbait was rather coarser than the earlier bags that I had bought. A new, improved recipe perhaps? I certainly didn't like it. It smelled different from previous bags too. One other change

that I had made was to buy some blood-worm and joker, in readiness for what I thought might be a hard match. I would soon find out if the small fish were in the vicinity or not.

On the whistle, I put in my usual five balls of feed and followed them in with the gozzer-baited pole tackle. I was ready for the instant bite, but was rather surprised to land a dace of a hundred grams or so. It was a start, but unlikely to be the leader of a shoal. The pit was towing very strongly from right to left. That is, directly opposite to the wind direction. In spite of this, I fed casters and hemp slightly to my right, in the hope that the wind and pull would cancel themselves out on the shallower top shelf.

For half an hour I persevered with the pole and maggot before trying a blood-worm on the hook. This attracted bites straight away but I was unable to hit them. I suspected that the culprits were too small to be of any use as a match winning force. The hemp and caster line also failed to generate a single bite. After an hour, it looked to be developing into a hard match.

Eventually, I managed to pick up a few small roach on the bloodworm, plus some tiny perch. At less than thirty grams each, all they were doing was keeping me active. Reluctantly, I decided to switch to the open-ended feeder. Bankside intelligence suggested that most anglers were now on the method but with nothing to show for it. My first cast dropped the feeder right on to the money – a real piece of luck in view of the strong wind and difficult casting conditions imposed by the geography of my peg. The feeder had not long settled before a bite was signalled on the quivertip and I struck into a half-kilo skimmer. This perked me up a lot and, with three hours still left, I felt confident of adding to my total. Unfortunately, I could not attract another bite, although a big booming line bite, when a fish swam into the line, nearly caused me to fall off my seat with surprise.

Obviously, there were a few fish out there, but they were showing little inclination to feed. Just into the final hour, I had a welcome visitor in the shape of Pete Vernon. However, the news that he brought was not good. Steve Yeomans was catching small fish, very regularly, from a peg further along my bank. Obviously, there were a few around him, but I was interested to know what he was doing differently. The main difference was his size 22 hook and 0.34kg hooklink. Although I couldn't see it making much difference to my catch rate, I changed down from the size 20 to 0.45kg that I had been using as insurance against bigger fish.

Pete had only been gone about five minutes when I had a bite on the double bloodworm-loaded size 22. I lifted into an unforeseen snag that surprised me by moving slowly out towards the centre of the pit. I had only seen the float for a fraction of a second as I lifted into the bite, and now, with the size 3 Zim elastic streaming into the depths of the lake, it looked as though I would never see it again. Fortunately, the fish did not rush off like a mad thing and I was easily able to keep pace by adding sections to my pole until I was playing it at eleven metres.

Restrained by the breaking strain of my hooklink, I kept up as much pressure as I could on the fish, which I was now convinced was a tench in the kilo range – big enough to give me the run-around, but not big enough to take me into the frame. Slowly, the fish swam to my right, which suited me well as it was battling against a strong underwater tow. Before it went too far, I was able to turn it around and lead it back towards me. The fish circled in front of me for several long minutes, before making a more spirited bid for freedom, again swimming against the stream to my

right. This time the elastic just kept going and going. I had the pole at full arm's length with the tip being pulled below the surface of the water and I expected the hooklink to give up the ghost.

Miraculously, the fish stopped in its tracks and again came back into its favourite position directly in front of me. I sensed the fish was tiring and began to take joints off my pole, increasing the pressure to lift the fish from the bottom. For the first time in what seemed like an age, my float came back into view. The fish still wasn't finished, though, and tried determinedly to get back to the bottom. The joints had to be put back on again. This time, however, there was no bid for freedom and the fish seemed content to lurch around at eleven metres.

Putting the pressure on again resulted in the fish coming towards the surface, and, while it was still a couple of metres down, I was able to see what I was attached too. It was a bream that I would have been happier to catch on the swimfeeder gear. The last few moments were an anti-climax. Unshipping joints smoothly, I worked the bream into netting range and landed it with little fuss. It had taken me twenty-five minutes to land it, and I have never had a bream fight so hard for so long. The size 22 hook was lodged tightly in the corner of its mouth and I could have played the fish until Christmas without it falling off the hook. In case of a repeat performance, I replaced the hook with the previous size 20.

There was now slightly less than half an hour of the match remaining, and it was in no confident mood that I dropped the pole tackle in again in search of another bite. Once again the float slid away and an unhurried lift met with weighty resistance. However, this was no monster, and at half a kilo this skimmer was swiftly landed. I now thought that I was on for a grand finale, but in the event I only added a

John Harper with his 35kg catch of chub, barbel and dace from peg 47 on the River Dove. I drew it and failed dismally.

few more small roach before the whistle sounded.

The big skimmer on its own weighed exactly 2kg – a decent bonus fish – and it boosted my weight to 3kg 60g giving me another second placing. The timely bream had just enabled me to pip Steve Yeomans by 50g. It was a pretty close call. However, this might have been another match that got away. When I didn't get any more bites from bream in the last twenty minutes or so, I should perhaps have tried the open-ended feeder dropped in a few yards to my left, on the line of the groundbait that I had

put in. It could be that the disturbance of landing those two fish had caused the shoal to drop downstream slightly, out of reach of the pole. The feeder may have been the answer.

Be that as it may, I was more than pleased with the results that I was getting on that venue, and was obviously having a run of fortune with decent bream at crucial times. I thought my luck was really in on a River Dove Open when I drew one of the best pegs on the river – peg 47. I was counting my winnings mentally as I made my way to the area. The fence end swim

The small balsa that I set up in the forlorn hope of catching barbel on the River Dove. Another home-made special, from a design pinched from Loughborough's Ron Stacey. At only 5cm long, there is plenty of room to put shots on to the line – a vital float on some of the shallow swims on the upper Trent.

runs on to a scour and holds dace, chub, barbel and the odd nuisance pike. Although there was a tricky downstream wind and the river had a drop of extra water in it, I still fancied my chances of a big weight. The safe option is to fish for dace on a stick float, with a ten-kilo catch a real possibility. But if the barbel show, they can be almost impossible to land on dace tackle, and disrupt things when they come on to the feed. The swim also has a resident pike that often embarks on dace snatching raids; this too causes problems.

An overhanging willow on the far bank provides cover for the chub shoal that is normally in residence, and although these can sometimes be caught on a stick float

fished towards the middle of the river, they normally fall to waggler tactics. The real maestro on this peg is John Harper, who has drawn it on several occasions and won in style every time, the most notable being a 35kg haul in a DFDS match a couple of years previously. I decided to go for broke on this match as such an opportunity does not normally present itelf. Because of this I opted to ignore the easy eight or nine kilos of dace and to fish for barbel and chub. My barbel tackle consisted of an old Ashurst carbon float rod, with 1.5kg reel line direct to a forged 18 feeder hook. The float was a small balsa bulk shotted with six fours and a couple of droppers below this. On the line that I would be fishing, I found around a metre and a half of water – ideal.

The waggler rig was also fairly simple – a 2 SSSG inserted waggler set at two metres, 1kg mainline to 0.75kg hooklink and a size 18 hook. I decided to fish casters rather than maggots as I thought that this would give me a better chance of barbel. I also thought that the chub would take anything that I threw at them. Three litres of hemp and the same of casters made up my bait for the day. The fish were not going to go short of feed on this occasion.

I decided to start off on the balsa rig and straight away, I was in trouble. Dace bites plagued me right from the start, and although I caught one or two they did not hang on for too long with the bulk-shotted rig. After an hour of trying various com-binations of bait, two or three casters at a time instead of one, and altering the depth to drag bottom even harder, I did not have a barbel to show for my troubles, and less than a kilo of dace.

Surely the chub would respond on the waggler line. I had been feeding this from the off, but again it was dace that responded to the feed. After about twenty minutes on the waggler, I was catching dace steadily but had not landed a chub. The closest that

River Dove waggler set-up.

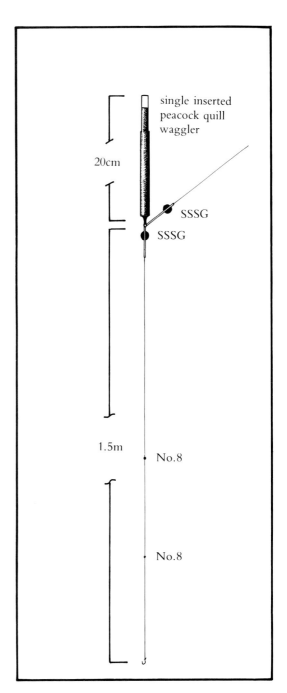

single inserted
peacock quill
waggler

20cm

SSSG

SSSG

1.5m

No.8

No.8

My River Dove waggler – a simple, inserted peacock quill job.

I had come was hooking one after about fifteen minutes on the method, only to have it throw the hook at the net. It looked to be around the kilo mark and would have been a nice bonus.

Eventually, the dace cooled off on the waggler line, but still no chub came to the net. Again I switched to the balsa, having been feeding the inside heavily with hemp and a few casters. Still I had problems with dace and no barbel to show for my efforts.

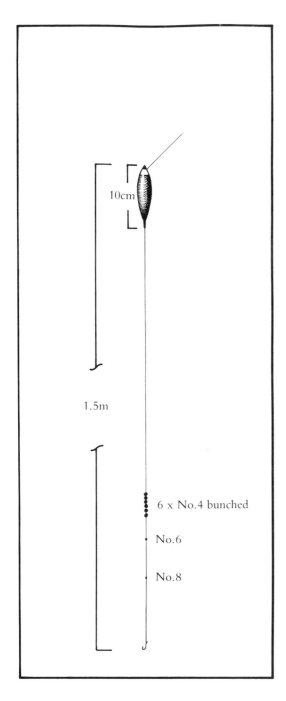

10cm

1.5m

6 x No.4 bunched

No.6

No.8

River Dove balsa rig. It failed miserably on this match, but a similar set-up caught me 22 kilos of chub in the same match that John Harper won with 35kg.

With time ticking away, I decided to stick it out on the waggler for the remaining two hours. The dace came and went on a whim and it was not until half an hour from the end that I, at last, caught a couple of chub, although they were not big fish and would have struggled to make a kilo between them. I finished the match totally dispirited with 4.5kg of hard-caught dace on the waggler.

John McCarthy's tactics had let me down. I should have played the percentages on this one and set up a stickfloat rig to start with. Only ten kilos won the match, and I am sure that I could have got close to that if only I had fished for dace instead of chasing shadows. If I had not won the match, I would have been guaranteed a pick up of some sort. I only needed another kilo for a section win. Not even to get into the frame from this peg was absolutely heart rending, and I felt far worse about it than failing at Kings Langley on the Grand Union a couple of months later. I will not make that mistake again.

However, the majority of anglers on the day said that they would have gone for the big weight in exactly the same manner, and come unstuck. At least they had benefited without it costing them an opportunity. As for the anglers who said that they would have naturally started on the stickfloat for the dace, I could only bow to their greater knowledge, and hope that they drew the peg on a day when twenty kilos of waggler-caught chub was on the cards!

A team match on the Drakelow section saw me drawn just above an area that I really fancied. However, I was sure that under the perfect river conditions I could manage a five kilo catch of roach that would put me well up in the section. The method that I based this plan on was the waggler, and it has seldom failed me in the past when conditions have been anything like perfect.

A slimmer insert than normal on this peacock quill waggler. I decided on this particular pattern as I had roach in mind.

I took a gamble and set up only one rod, although I knew that there was a chance of catching a few fish on the stick float from my peg. The anglers around me, strangers to the venue, had set up a wide array of methods – stickfloats, wagglers, swimfeeders and roachpoles. This was exactly what I needed if my plan was to work. In past matches on that length, I had often started off very slowly on the waggler before starting to put a few fish together. However, once started, the fish seem to feed very well, so I was naturally confident that the more I concentrated on this one method, the greater my reward would be. Because of this, I was not too surprised to start the match quite slowly, although I was slightly worried about the depth that I had on the waggler line. At close to three metres, I felt that it might be a little too deep for a summer match.

I decided to use a two swan waggler with a fairly slender insert, again of peacock quill. No groundbait was going to be catapulted into the swim this time, just maggots and hemp seed, although I did have some cereal groundbait with me as a precaution. The river was running quite steadily so three eights and one six were all the shot that I needed down the line. Had the swim been a metre or so shallower I would have dispensed with the one number 6, and also one of the number 8s. On the business end, I had a size 20 hook to 0.45kg nylon.

My first fish, a small roach, came after about fifteen minutes – a good early sign. However, its relatives seemed very reluctant to join it in the keepnet. The angler downstream of me had also started the match on the waggler, but had made the common error of fishing with a float that was far too light for a river such as the upper Trent. He was not only struggling to cast the float the required distance, but also to keep it there, the slightest bow in his line pulling it off course.

He had more luck when he switched to the stick float and netted a roach of around a third of a kilo. This put him ahead of me, and although I switched to a size 22 and 0.35kg hooklink, my swim stayed quite dead. Half of the match had passed before I decided that desperate measures were required. I stopped feeding altogether just on a hunch that the fish might want a bit of a rest. However, I wasn't surprised when the response was nil.

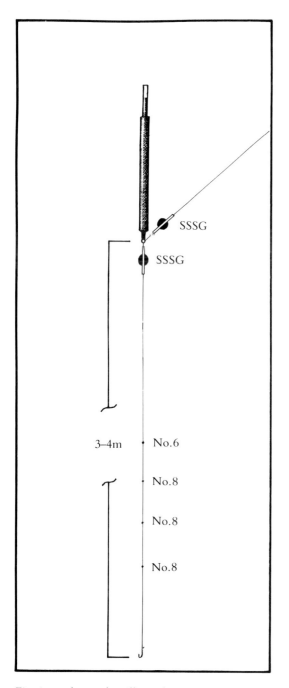

Fine inserted peacock quill waggler.

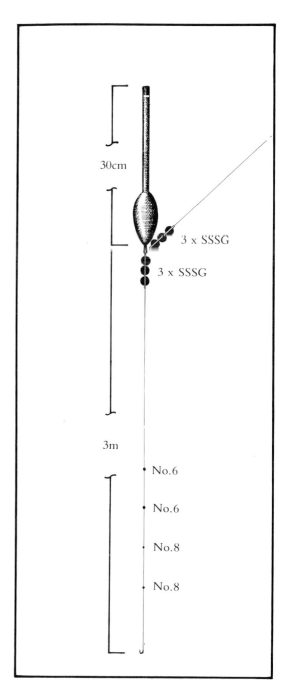

Big peacock quill and balsa waggler for fishing at extreme range.

I knew that if I was struggling, others would be too. However, it was starting to look as though I had dug myself a bit of a hole that would take some getting out of. Feeding the waggler line again did not make a scrap of difference so, with a couple of hours to go, I decided to tackle up a different rod. This was not a stick float rod (I had passed the stage where I could have caught up with anyone who had a start on me), but a heavy waggler rig. I was opposite an area where bream had been caught on the waggler occasionally, so I decided to try for these.

I put an open-faced reel loaded with 1.5kg line on this rod. The reason for this was that I intended to use a very big float. At thirty centimetres long and with a big balsa body, the peacock quill waggler carried the amount of shotting needed to cast the distance. Locked on each side with 3SSSG shot, I was still able to get away with only a couple of sixes and eights down the line. I had a couple of practice runs with the big float to establish the line that I could fish comfortably and the depth to set the float at, and I was ready for action. The depth as far as I could cast, was still three metres which, in this case, helped, as I was going to use cereal groundbait, heavy stuff at that. I knocked up a couple of kilos of brown bread crumb, Beet and Kanal, and added a litre of casters and a sprinkling of squatts, formed half a dozen cricket balls of feed and hurled them across the river.

Naturally, this caused a good deal of ribald comment from the anglers in the vicinity, but, by landing the waggler right on the feed line, I was at least able to illustrate that I intended to fish that area. On the first run down the float dipped and dragged its way along until it reached the spot where I estimated any interested fish would be lying. Magically, it slid confidently away. Picking up the bow in the line, I settled the rod into a nice skimmer.

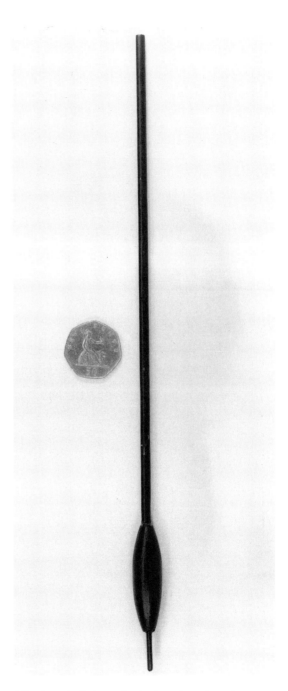

This large-bodied waggler is about three times the size of a normal Trent float but desperate situations require desperate measures. At 6 SSSG plus, it still isn't the biggest float that I have had to resort to on the Drakelow section.

A half-kilo fish was just what the doctor ordered as a starter and I felt confident of a repeat prescription. Unfortunately, it turned out to be a shell-shocked singleton, although I greatly enjoyed the opportunity to fish the big waggler at range. I suppose I was showing off really.

At the end of the match, I weighed in just under a kilo, beating the angler downstream of me, but about half a kilo behind the next angler upstream. He had fished the bulk of the match on the stick float, picking up a few fish here and there. But, on his first cast on the waggler he had picked up a roach very nearly as big as my skimmer. Strangely, this too was a lone fish. Whatever else I had learned it had certainly not been a day for the waggler. Also, it had been the first time that the loose feed method had let me down. However, the river in my area had not fished well at all. The cock peg running on to the railway bridge had only come up with 6kg, with the gravel pegs above it only producing about half their potential, or perhaps rather less.

The rest of the team had similarly poor days, and it was clear that we had not had a very good draw. However, at least I had another round of the summer league on the River Trent to look forward to. On this round, the section included the same peg on which I had come second to Roy Duckett all those years previously. However, the main shoaling point for bream is now some five or six pegs above this, although naturally there is a chance of a skimmer or two from most of the pegs in that area.

Strangely enough, I had not drawn on any quantity of bream on this section, since my second placing, usually having to fish for roach for reasonable team points. Plenty of practice sessions in the area had given me confidence on the bream, but I had not had the chance to display my skills in

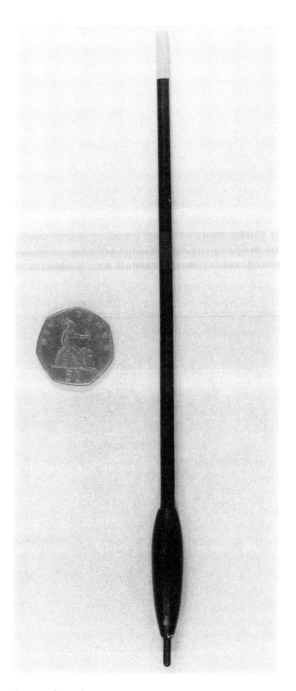

Nice and simple – a bodied waggler for extra distance and control on the upper Trent. Normally, I would have chosen a float without a body, but, with the river out of sorts, I had to compromise to get anything like the correct presentation.

public. This time, the draw saw me smack in the reed bed area, right where the bream should be. However, it appeared that I was towards the downstream end, some distance away from where the bream normally show. This didn't worry me too much as I had a feeling that the bream might have moved downstream slightly. I had practised on the hot pegs mid-week and caught only a couple of bream. These had come very late in the day and had convinced me that the shoal was not on the normally favoured pegs. The question was, would they be on mine?

This was soon answered. The team (John Harper, Derek Jackson, Pete Vernon and myself), carried out the usual pre-match rundown of our pegs and what results we hoped for. Going methods were discussed, recent form, new ideas, the normal team jargon. I remained silent until asked where I thought I was drawn. I was hoping that no one would ask following my humbling experience on the Dove Open. However, ask they did, and when I told them they seemed satisfied that I might do a reasonable team job. The only slight niggle was that John Harper told me that a club match had been fished on the section the previous day and 24kg had won the match – from my peg. This was the sort of information that I didn't want to hear. I could not believe that the bream would take a pounding two days running. With my spirits appreciably lowered, I set off for my peg.

One advantage of the area is that it entails only a short walk, and on the day in question this was a real bonus. The rain was bucketing down, and my first job on arriving at my peg was to set my umbrella up – not to shelter under, but to keep my tackle and bait dry. I had no wish for my three litres of maggots to make a mass escape or change into floaters. I wasn't fishing for carp this time.

Alrewas canal ace 'Digger' Bailey was on the next peg when I won the third round match of the summer league. Afterwards, he bought me a drink because he thought that my performance deserved it. I wonder how many sports there are where that would happen.

I set up only two rigs – a waggler and a swimfeeder. The stick float has no history of reasonable weights from the peg that I was drawn on. However, the river did appear to be carrying a few inches of extra water, and there was an added hazard in the form of rafts of floating weed to contend with. In spite of this, I decided to start the match on the swimfeeder to try to pick up any simple bream that happened to be in the swim. I had, by now, decided that the initial heavy feed for bream was a big gamble, especially since they had been hammered the day before. I opted to put in just what groundbait would fit into a feeder, deciding on a size 18 to 0.75kg hooklink with a redworm as the starting bait.

Another unusual choice was my decision

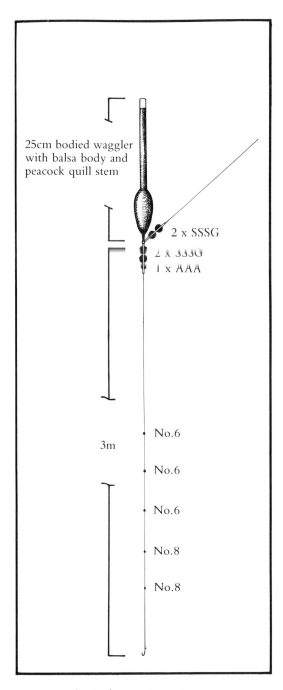

25cm bodied waggler with balsa body and peacock quill stem

2 x SSSG

2 x SSSG
1 x AAA

3m

No.6

No.6

No.6

No.8

No.8

Heavy waggler rig for upper Trent bream.

to drop the feeder here and there in the swim, hoping to put it close enough to a bream to encourage a bite, rather than dropping it in the same spot and waiting for them to come to it. After the previous day's mauling, I thought that they might not be in the mood to travel too far. My groundbait was the now almost standard mix of brown crumb and Beet. I had dispensed with the Kanal by this time, it being a little too binding under some circumstances. I did not want to give these bream shell-shock. Again I had a litre each of casters and squatts to put into the groundbait.

Forty five minutes on the feeder attracted nil response to my redworm hookbait, although, in between casts, I had been preparing a waggler swim by catapulting maggots about four rod lengths out. When I switched to the waggler, it was to a rather heavier rig than normal as I was using a bodied peacock waggler with no insert. This was locked with 4SSSG shots and an AAA, although I had only three sixes and two eights down the line. The heavier float was used in order that I could slow its progress down in the style of a stick float, without pulling it off line.

It was sensitive enough to register a bite from a gudgeon, which was my first fish and saved me the embarrassment of a dry net. Another brace of gudgeon swiftly followed, plus a roach of around a hundred grams. I was not catching much, but, from what I could see of the anglers downstream of me, I was still well in contention as the river looked to be fishing very hard indeed.

Because of the continuous rain, I was not wearing my bait apron and had to reach under my umbrella to fill the pouch of my catapult if I wished to loose feed. This meant that I was not firing maggots into the swim at every cast, but around one in three or four. However, I was throwing a small egg-sized ball of groundbait out on

A reverse tapered peacock quill waggler. Ideal for dragging hard on, in quickly flowing water.

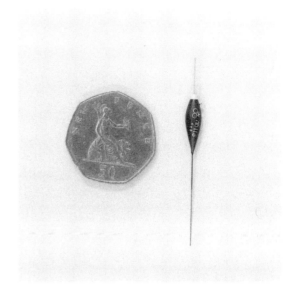

This was the smallest float in my box, but it proved ideal for catching fry on what was a very trying day.

to the waggler line every alternate cast, so at least some feed was going into my swim.

About an hour and a quarter of the match had passed when the waggler once again dragged slowly under. This time the strike met with a solid resistance that let me know I had hooked a bream. With a drop of extra water, the current really gave the fish something to grab on to as it turned broadside-on to the flow. However, I was able to guide it out of the main current and through the reed beds that made a barrier to my peg about three metres from the bank. Once I had it my side of the nearly

submerged weeds, the rest was easy and I gently shepherded the fish towards my waiting landing net.

Then the hook pulled out, and several points worth of bream slipped back into the current and freedom. The fish looked to be just over half a kilo and would have given me a real boost. Under the circumstances, I could not hope for a repeat performance. However, my luck was in and within ten minutes I had a fish of similar size on the hook and in the net. From what I could see, this put me ahead of all the anglers on the pegs downstream, but my jubilation was tempered with a note of caution when I saw the angler next door bend into a bream on the swimfeeder. Until that point he had been biteless. What the anglers upstream were doing, I could not tell as the dense reed beds obscured my vision.

Another fifteen minutes passed and I latched into bream number two. This was very much bigger at a kilo and a half and seemed to kite around at thirty metres for an eternity before I was able to persuade it to give up the struggle. The size of that fish and the problems that it had given me decided me to try the swimfeeder again. This time, though, I baited the hook with two red maggots, instead of the normal redworm. I had caught both fish on the waggler with maggots on the hook. With the landing of that first bream, the weather had also improved – the rain stopped, the sun shone, and all in the garden was lovely. I began to enjoy myself.

My first cast with the feeder in its second spell saw me striking at the merest tremble of the tip. Again there was a hefty thump and soon I had a trio of bream in the net – guaranteed good points, especially in view of the size of the second fish. As in the previous round, I had started with a tail of around one metre between feeder and hook, but this had now been lengthened to just shy of two metres. In my mid-week practice session I had finished up fishing the swimfeeder with a three-metre tail to attract bites – very difficult to cast, but better than attracting no bites at all.

Perhaps the bream on this section are getting wiser. Certainly I thought that a longer tail must be a good bet after the previous day's carnage, and I would have duplicated the mid-week rig if need be. Why the bream showed a preference for the red maggot hookbait, I do not know. Digger Bailey, on the downstream peg, was catching his fish on caster, so there may be some significance in that. However, although I am quite fond of caster as a bream bait in some situations, I thought that the red maggot might stand up to the attentions of the gudgeon, that were evident, rather better than the caster.

Another point that convinced me of their worth was the fact that I was putting red squatts into the groundbait. This took my mind back to one end-of-season day on Willesley Lake when I caught a couple of

bream early and then could not attract another bite for some two hours. Finally, I baited up with a couple of red pinkies, and miraculously, the bites came again. I finished up with a nice net of fish. As it was only a practice session, I alternated with other baits to see if there was a difference. The red pinkie was the only one that the fish would look at. Although I stop short of using some of the rather livid red groundbaits that some anglers favour for bream, I can see that, under some circumstances, they can have their uses. (I think that on that day at Willesley, I had used some of the Sensas Red 272 in my groundbait as an experiment, but I have not continued with it as it has let me down a couple of times since.)

The next two casts produced identically tentative bites, but I was able to spot them and took my tally to five. I was at the half-way stage in the match and felt that I had it sewn up. Although I had picked up some nice fish, the only additional feed that I was putting into my swim was going in via my swimfeeder. I knew that this was not much to hold a shoal of fish, but, as I was catching odd ones, I decided not to feed anything else which might scatter them.

Bites took some time to develop, however, and it was not the normally fast and furious bream sport that comes when they are well on the feed. I sensed that the shoal would be easily unsettled. The fact that they had drifted to the next angler downstream a couple of times confirmed this. He was still stuck on two fish having lost one at the net. Three or four casts without a bite decided me to have another dip with the waggler. Really, the last thing that I wanted to do was have the trouble of playing another fish on float tackle in that current, but at least I would be doing something constructive whilst resting the swim from the impact of a swimfeeder. I was also interested to find out whether or not the bream had dropped downstream away from the catching area.

With that in mind, I decided that the fifteen blank minutes on the float was time well spent. As far as I could tell, the bream were still on the feeder line, at the head of the swim – a difficult area to fish properly on waggler tackle. With exactly two hours left, I again switched to the swimfeeder. This time the sport was hectic, with seven fish in the next hour putting me safely (I thought), ahead of the field. However, the bites were still tentative. Not the nice drop backs that I expected but rather a vague quiver of the rod tip.

Going into the last hour with a dozen bream safely in my net, I began to think of breaking records. However, the bream had other ideas and again bites ceased. A switch to worm brought no response, and three or four casts on the waggler would not reveal their whereabouts. Now the angler downstream of me picked up a couple of quick fish on the feeder. I knew that he now had four in his net, and perhaps the rest of the shoal in his swim. Looking at my watch, I saw that he needed to land another eight in the remaining thirty minutes to equal me in numbers of bream caught. I did not fancy his chances.

I decided to put in another couple of balls by hand, the first since the early part of the match. These were almost tennis-ball sized. I knew that the bream were not in front of me, and took a gamble that a few particles of feed wafting enticingly downstream might bring them back. It did. I attracted another three bites for two fish, losing one in the near side reeds. It was only a small fish but I was annoyed at myself for losing it. It had come in so fast that I suspected it might make a last dash for freedom amongst the reeds. It did, and I still couldn't prevent it from getting into them. The hook pulled just as I persuaded it to come out.

My last fish came just nicely as the final whistle sounded, and was on its way to the net as the anglers around me were tackling down. The angler downstream of me had seen me land only five fish, and the angler upstream had not a clue as to what I had caught. I conservatively estimated my catch at 7kg (half a kilo per fish), but privately I thought that they might go a bit more. They did, and with a final total of 12kg, I doubled the weight of the runner-up. At last I had laid to rest the ghost of that second placing all those years previously.

True, the field was not quite as star-studded as it had been on that day, and I had again drawn an outstanding peg. However, the result was very different. I had beaten more than a hundred other anglers, and beaten them in style. That was the final lesson taught me by the four anglers whom I studied, and it is a nice note to end on.

The last match with Sammy Mann taught me that the finest technique in the world cannot help if you are not on fish. He had already taught me the value of preparation and practice in staying one jump ahead. In Dickie Carr's case, I learned that a peg that you really fancy can sometimes let you down, and you have to be man enough to accept the inevitable criticism that comes because of it. John McCarthy taught me the value of perseverance in the face of adversity, whilst well off the pace on a big-weight venue. Similarly, Nigel Bull taught me that (especially on canals), a no-hope peg can sometimes spring a nice surprise.

They all taught me that the next cast could be the one that sees the match swing your way. They reinforced these lessons time and again through their attitude, dedication and self-belief, but above all, they taught me how to win.

8 Summing Up

Winning the third round of the summer league match helped our team to second place in the league. However, we still had to beat the leaders, by at least one place, in the final match to secure the title.

This time, I drew on a gravel straight on the Drakelow section, an area that I didn't fancy for good section points, the best area being the run down to the Leicester line railway bridge. The area that I was drawn in has a reputation for very poor results whatever match is fished on the venue. Why, I don't know, because it looks as though it ought to be full of roach. On the day in question, the river was carrying extra water, and rising – hardly ideal for a gravel run. However, at the start I decided to fish the stick float, as this looked to be the best chance of catching a fish, always a difficult prospect under conditions such as this. Because of the extra flow, and to be able to search the river further out, I decided upon a six number four Lignum stick (home-made). I also set up a waggler rod and a swimfeeder set up just in case. The waggler was a straight peacock float locked by 2 SSSG and 1 AAA, and had a reverse taper. I wanted to slow the bait down as much as possible.

I didn't use the bodied pattern on this occasion because the river was rather higher, and I felt that the extra current would have grabbed hold of the balsa body rather more and made tackle control difficult. On the swimfeeder front, I set up a block end rather than open end. I was expecting chub not bream to figure on that method.

I started the match on the stick float, and, right from the start, it was clear that this was going to be a difficult day. Floating weed festooned the shots at every cast, and one cast in a dozen met with the float encountering a really large mat of weed which prevented it from cocking altogether. In spite of this, I managed to attract a bite after twenty minutes' hard labour and swung a gudgeon to hand. I did not realise at the time how vital this early fish would be. A short while later Swadlincotes' Sam Hicks, who had the benefit of a large bay downstream of him sheltering him from the worst of the weed, latched into a useful perch of a hundred and fifty grams or so.

So far as I could gather, not much else was being caught. Certainly my swim had now deteriorated to the extent that a bite on any method looked unlikely. A few casts on the waggler revealed the impossibility of that method, with the swimfeeder similarly hopeless. The floating weed wrapped itself around the line almost as soon as the feeder hit bottom. Landing a decent fish would have been a hard prospect. Persisting with the stick float, I saw that Sam had again struck into a fish, this time a chub of around four hundred grams. As far as I could see, he might have been winning the section.

With three hours of the match left, I decided upon a desperate gamble. The thirty or so centimetres of water that I was standing in appeared to harbour a few small fry, especially in the area of slack created by my keepnet. I decided to increase this area of

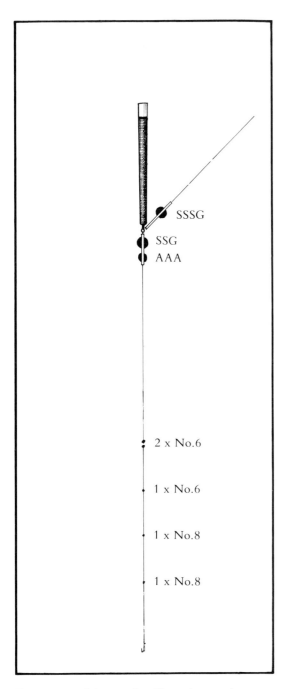

Reverse taper plain peacock quill waggler set to drag hard on.

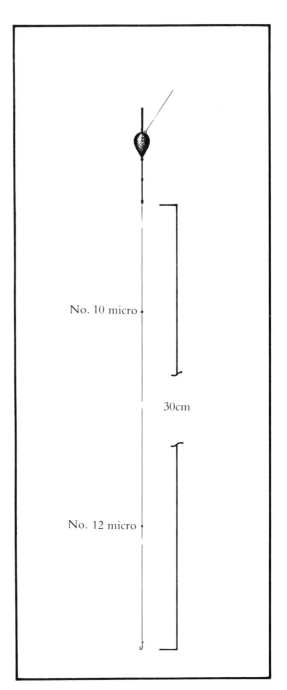

4 x 9 milo miniature pole float. A real tiddler-snatching rig.

slack by jamming my umbrella into the gravel just upstream of my peg. This had the desired effect. All I now had to do was catch those fish.

I set up a five-metre pole rig complete with the tiniest float that I could find, plus a size 30 hook to 0.11kg nylon. My bait was a single, very shrunken pinkie. I had kept some in my bait fridge for eight or ten weeks against such an eventuality and they had shrunk a great deal from their original size. Straight away, I began to pick up tiny fish, sticklebacks in the main, but also a few minnows, tiny dace and chub.

Why did I do such a crazy footling **thing** as fish for fry? I had a few reasons, the most important being that if I could catch enough of them, I would be in with a chance of beating all of the other anglers who had caught just one gudgeon. I might even be able to beat the anglers who had caught two or three of them, and every point was going to be vital on this day. Also, it was keeping me interested, and, with my area of slack water well established on a very coloured river, there was always the chance that one or two proper fish might find their way into it.

I caught well until half an hour from the end when bites ceased almost completely. However, I had picked up three nearly proper dace of around fifteen grams apiece so I was well pleased. Stories of my tactics had spread along the section by the end of the match, with the result that most anglers had a stickleback or two to weigh in. However, they had obviously left it far too late to be in with any chance of catching up with me after giving me a minimum of an hour's start. At the weigh-in, I came sixth in the section, beaten by all of the anglers with a few real fish, four of them being drawn on the run towards the bridge. Sam was the only other angler to beat me and he was only fifth with a good half kilo. We had clearly been drawn in the wrong area.

On the day, I was king of the fry anglers, although Derby's Dennis Hagues was only about thirty grams behind me! The only unfortunate note was Doug Fisher of Alrewas winning our section comfortably with a couple of skimmers for a kilo and a half. His was the team that we had to beat. On the next section down, Pete Vernon had fished a heroic match to take second in his section with one fish, a heart-stopping kilo-and-a-half bream taken on the waggler less than an hour from the finish.

Derek Jackson had also done well, but we feared bad news from John Harper who only had a couple of gudgeon to weigh in. We fancied that we might be second on the day to the league leaders, to finish second overall. Incredibly, we won the match by a single point, with John's catch being one of very few that were weighed in on his section. Alrewas were unlucky to finish third on the day behind Sam Hicks' team, giving us the league title in the process.

The real icing on the cake, as far as I am concerned, is that both myself and Derek Jackson have been in teams that have won this title on several occasions, numbering John and Pete amongst our victims each time. It really has been our lucky series so far, at John's and Pete's expense, so it was a real bonus to be able to win it with them in the team and contributing to our success.

All of the anglers that I have covered in this book continue to go from strength to strength. Dickie Carr is still getting a few nice little earners on the River Lea, John McCarthy is picking up a placing in the Aikens pole championship (*on a canal!*), Sammy Mann is still doing his stuff for the Keenets Aquarians and last, but not least, Nigel Bull is still winning, most recently with a stunning twenty-nine kilos of bream from the River Trent. Not on the feeder, however – stick float and casters.

9 What of The Future?

One of the tantalising aspects of watching good anglers at work is that they make it look so easy, and by 'it', I mean everything. To the average match angler this probably means very little, but don't you believe it. If you want a graphic illustration of the difference between them and us, take a novice out with you for a few days and see how rough they look. The greats exude an oil of confidence which lubricates their every move.

They are fast without looking fast, because they do everything with a remarkable economy of effort. One of the best examples of this art was Pete Palmer fishing the waggler. The more fish he caught, the slower he seemed to get, to the extent that you almost thought that he was putting the fish back into the river. However, at the end of the match, he always seemed to have lots more fish than anyone else. I well remember no lesser angler than Wayne Swinscoe returning after a match on the Trent with the kind of expression on his face that you used to see on a particularly harrowing kind of NSPCC poster. Obviously everyone wanted to know what had happened to him. His reply was 'I've been Palmered!' That said it all.

What has that got to do with the future? Well, because they make it look so easy, it is very tempting to get drawn back into competitive angling on a large scale. Far from making you think thoughts like 'I could never do that', they make you think thoughts like 'I don't know what all the fuss is about'. It is very easy to fall into the same trap when watching something like the London Marathon. It looks easy until you have a go.

This isn't the only temptation that can lead you back on to the open circuit. There is also the camaraderie. Ninety per cent of match anglers know that they are in the same boat on any given match, namely, that they aren't going to win anything that day, and so they go to enjoy the day for its own sake.

They can also be very generous – not only in talking about winning methods, but at the matches themselves. A couple of instances spring to mind. One is Nigel Bull letting me have some bloodworm that he had spent a lot of time and effort scraping, on a team match (relax, it wasn't the Angling Times Winter League), because I had been badly let down by my supplier. Another is Dennis Hagues similarly free-handed with a few lobworms on a rain swollen River Trent. Also, as I mentioned with Sammy Mann, a lot of anglers are genuinely pleased to see you win, especially if you are not one of the big names. After that summer league match on the River Trent that I won, Digger Bailey bought me a drink, simply because he said that my performance on the day had been worth it. That simple gesture meant more to me than the money that I picked up. However, I have a feeling that if I ever draw next to Digger in a canal match, then it will be me who is standing the drinks. It will be my pleasure.

On the other side of the coin, you can sometimes get adverse comments, even when you win. There is generally someone who thinks that they could have done it so much better, and maybe they could. But so what? You took your chance and won, and for every angler like this there will be a dozen more who will want to shake your hand. Having been on the scene before also gives a different view of things. Of course a run of poor draws still gets frustrating, but, with the benefit of experience, you realise that as the world turns, it is of little significance. When reigning Wimbledon Champion, Boris Becker, was knocked out in an early round the next year, he was very philosophical. 'Nobody got killed, nobody lost a war, I just lost a tennis match.' An admirable attitude and one that it would do us well to remember.

Sometimes, under adverse conditions, the angler's only aim is to salvage his own self-esteem with catching all that he can from the peg that he has drawn. Really it is the anglers who are interested enough to do this who will go a long way. That is one reason why it can be well worthwhile travelling around on the open circuit rather than staying too close to home. It is easier to work hard on an unknown venue than a familiar one. On the former a poor draw will still be very much an unknown quantity; on the latter you can be beaten before you start. I know, I've been there.

Another worry is what to do if you draw next to a really big name, or rather, what will happen? The answer to the latter question is easier to answer – either you will beat him, or he will beat you. (A tie on weight will give you a moral victory, however!) Whatever the outcome you will be better for it. It is worth remembering that you have nothing to lose. They can be beaten, and you only have to do it once to know that you can do it again. Not every time maybe, but sometimes. I have beaten all the subjects of this book either off the next peg, or the next but one. The most recent was last season when I managed to get a verdict over Nigel Bull at the second peg along. There were only a few grams in it, and Nigel had been unlucky to lose a decent roach, but I had had one of those matches when I hadn't lost a fish, and that was good enough.

For the first time in ages I decided to breed a few gozzers for the odd match in the season. Did they give me an edge? Well, I did catch a few timely skimmers, winning me more money than they had cost to produce. I also took the trouble to turn my own casters. Again, I was able to go to matches with a first class supply of bait, and I was enjoying the work involved. I began to put in some practice again – real practice, not just pleasure fishing – and it is surprising, how, under those circumstances it is possible to re-learn things that were once taken for granted. A lot of old memories also came flooding back – great and not so great days, names and places.

I think that I shall take another tentative dip in the waters of the open circuit, not because I have anything to prove but just for the recreational aspect. Perhaps if I had been so relaxed a few years ago, I might have tasted more of the fruits of success, but what is past is past. I asked John McCarthy if he still had the old fire in his belly, and he told me that it was more like embers now. Then again, they didn't need much fanning to bring them back to life. I think that I know what he means. Meeting some of the old faces put a new purpose into life. John Larraman was a case in point. The last time I had seen him was on the next peg on a River Trent open when we had drawn opposite the stone bridge in the Nelson Field at Burton Joyce. By a bizarre turn of fate, I beat him that day by landing a kilo and a half carp. Typically of all these anglers, he remembered it before I did. I got a sneaking feeling that he was hoping to draw next to me at Theale to get his own back!

Putting this book together took me around a few different venues and fuelled my interest again, not least because I was investing time, effort and hard-earned cash. If I was going to take the amount of bait that John McCarthy insisted I required at Theale, then I was certainly going to get my money's worth out of it! On the down side, this charging about must have had a disruptive effect, as believe it or not, it made it almost impossible to schedule my matches with any confidence. I am used to not knowing where I am, but this was a case of not knowing where I would be. Still, I was able to get a few results. Imagine what I might have done if I had put a proper season together. (Am I dreaming?)

There isn't too much of this season left to go now, but already I am starting to make a few plans for next year. I got lucky with bream this season, perhaps I can carry it on to the next one too. I also have a certain score to settle with the Grand Union Canal at Kings Langley. Minnows and all, it looked a very interesting venue. Then there is always Theale. I still like the odd challenge, and it is the ideal place to go if I happen to have a lot of bait left over anytime! I had forgotten how picturesque the River Avon can be, not to mention the

civilised draw times. Some of those canals don't look too bad either. There must be somewhere that the real canal aces haven't discovered yet, where I might be in with more of a shout.

It might be a little premature to get back into it so suddenly, and I can't see many of the open circuit regulars losing any sleep. However, each new season brings a new challenge. This season (1988), for the first time in years, it seemed as though the match circuit was buzzing again. Not just with keen newcomers (although there were plenty of them), but with former regulars who had caught the bug. I even heard that John Dean had been spotted fishing the River Trent again – not in matches, just for his own amusement (and others' amazement). Now that really would be a sight to see – J. D. back on the road. It would certainly be worth going along to watch him in action. I can't imagine that I will be drawing much of a crowd on my outings, but then again, that is the last thing that you want when you are catching a few.

The more anglers there are about, obviously, the harder it is going to be to win, but, to cater for them there will have to be more matches, more choice of venues, more opportunities. Who knows, I might do well enough to have someone want to write a book about me!

Index

Index